Prophetic Goal Setting:
Aligning Your Vision with God's Plan
2025 Edition

By Loxanne P. Taylor, Esq.

*"Write the vision and make it plain upon tablets,
that he may run that readeth it.
For the vision is yet for an appointed time,
but at the end it shall speak, and not lie."*

— **Habakkuk 2:2–3 (KJV)**

Prophetic Goal Setting: Aligning Your Vision with God's Plan
© 2025 Loxanne P. Taylor. All rights reserved.

All rights reserved. No part of this book may be reproduced, stored in a retrieval system, or transmitted in any form or by any means—electronic, mechanical, photocopying, recording, or otherwise—without prior written permission of the publisher, except for brief quotations used in reviews, articles, or educational works.

Scripture quotations are taken from the Holy Bible, King James Version (KJV) unless otherwise noted. Scripture quotations are used by permission and fall within fair use guidelines for non-commercial, limited quotation. No portion of this book reproduces a complete biblical book or an excessive number of verses from any translation. All rights reserved. Other Bible translations are identified and credited accordingly.

Published by Staten House

New York, New York

Cover design: "Designed by Author"

ISBN: 979-8-90243-001-8

Printed in the United States of America

Library of Congress Control Number: 2025927065

Taylor, Loxanne P.
  Prophetic Goal Setting: Aligning Your Vision with God's Plan
    by Loxanne P. Taylor
    p. cm.

Includes bibliographical references and index.

ISBN: 979-8-90243-001-8
  1. Christian life — Spiritual growth.
  2. Vision — Biblical teaching.
  3. Prophecy — Practical application.
  4. Goal setting — Religious aspects.

I. Title.

Legal Disclaimer

This book is intended for spiritual, educational, and inspirational purposes only. The teachings, insights, and recommendations offered herein are based on the author's understanding of biblical principles, personal experience, and prophetic interpretation.

This book does <u>not</u> provide legal, medical, financial, or psychological advice.

Readers should consult qualified professionals in those areas when needed.

While the author has made every effort to ensure the accuracy and clarity of the content, Loxanne P. Taylor and Staten House assume no responsibility for any actions taken by readers as a result of reading this book.

All personal examples, stories, and illustrations used are either fictionalized, used with permission, or adapted in ways that protect the privacy of individuals.

Use this material with prayer, discernment, and personal responsibility.

Dedication

To every visionary who dares to dream with God—
to the builders, intercessors, and believers who refuse to settle for an ordinary life—this book is dedicated to you.

May these pages remind you that your goals are not just plans; they are *prophetic invitations* from Heaven.

You are chosen, anointed, and empowered to walk boldly in divine purpose.
You are called to see, to believe, and to become everything God has spoken.

Keep trusting.
Keep building.
Keep saying yes.

Your destiny is not a distant hope—
it is unfolding right now in partnership with the Lord.

Acknowledgments

To Pastor Akeim Brown, thank you for shepherding me with unwavering spiritual care, the love of Jesus, prophetic insight, and Godly wisdom. Your leadership has trained my ears to discern God's voice clearly and my heart to obey Him without hesitation. I honor the grace you carry and the investment you continually make in my spiritual growth.

To Lady Coleisha Brown, thank you for your quiet strength, your encouragement, and your example of grace. Your experiential teachings, life principles, love, support, and wisdom have been a steadying force in my journey.

To Pastor Trevor Wallace and Bishop L. G. Johnson, I deeply appreciate your voices of wisdom, correction, and encouragement. Your counsel has grounded me, challenged me, and shaped the way I serve God's people. Thank you for pouring into my development with such faithfulness.

To my family and friends, thank you for being part of the soil God has used to form me. Even in seasons of challenge, difference, and stretching, God used each moment to refine my character and clarify the call on my life. Your presence in my journey is part of the testimony written on these pages.

And to every sister and brother in Christ who has prayed for me, spoken life over me, or shared a prophetic word at just the right time—this book is evidence of your intercession. Your prayers have watered the vision God placed in me, and

I am grateful.

With love and honor,

Loxanne P. Taylor

Preface

There comes a moment in every believer's life when simply wishing, hoping, or dreaming is no longer enough. There is a point where you must step into intentional partnership with God and become an active participant in what Heaven has spoken over you. That is where this book was born—in the space between revelation and responsibility.

For years, I watched believers receive powerful prophetic words, stirring visions, and Holy Spirit–inspired direction, yet struggle to walk them out in real life. Not because they lacked faith, but because they lacked clarity, structure, and understanding. We often celebrate the *moment* of prophecy but fail to embrace the *process* of manifestation.

God is not only a God who reveals—He is a God who builds. Jesus said, *"My Father is always working."* That means vision is only the beginning of the work God wants to do in your life.

This book is designed to help you:

- Understand what true, God-given vision is
- Discern the difference between a divine sight and human imagination
- Write the vision clearly and confidently
- Develop Spirit-led, strategic goals rooted in Scripture
- Execute with wisdom, discipline, and prophetic alignment
- Walk daily in purpose, clarity, and consistency

This is not a book of theory—it is a guide for transformation. It is a prophetic blueprint for believers who want to see what God has said and then *build* what God has shown.

As you read, I pray you will feel a fresh stirring in your spirit. I pray clarity will rise. I pray old dreams will be resurrected and new visions will awaken. And most importantly, I pray you will walk boldly into the plan God has prepared for you.

This is your moment.
This is your season of alignment.
This is your year to step into prophetic clarity and purposeful action.

Let's walk this journey together—one revelation, one step, one victory at a time.

My Journey Into Prophetic Goal Setting

My passion for Prophetic goal setting didn't begin in a classroom or a pulpit—it began at a simple vision board party with friends. We gathered to dream, to create, and to visualize what we hoped the coming year would bring. But by the end of that year, something remarkable had happened:

Almost everything I had placed on my vision board had come to pass.

I realized then that this was more than creativity or motivation—God was teaching me the power of strategic vision aligned with His purpose. That moment awakened something in me. I didn't want to simply hope for a good future; I wanted to be intentional. I wanted to cooperate with God's plans. I wanted to plan prophetically.

Year after year, my pastor entrusted me with the honor of teaching a Bible study on prophetic goal setting to our congregation. Through these sessions, I witnessed powerful testimonies and undeniable evidence of God at work.

- People began to see major God-sized business ideas come to fruition.
- Individuals and families experienced homeownership breakthroughs.
- Unmarried men and women stepped into God-ordained marriages.
- Ministries were birthed.
- Habits were broken.
- And clarity—deep, spiritual clarity—was released into the hearts of many.

The impact didn't stay local.
To my amazement, I was later invited to teach this prophetic goal setting framework at a government human resources department in a foreign country, and again at a church in that same foreign nation.

Doors opened that only God could open, confirming what I already knew:

This wasn't just a method.
This wasn't just a strategy.

This was a God-given blueprint that works anywhere His principles are honored.

Every testimony, every breakthrough, and every transformed life affirmed what the Holy Spirit taught me years ago at that vision board party:

> **When you align your sight with God's voice, Heaven backs your movement.**

That truth is the foundation of this book.

Table of Contents

Preface   ix
Introduction: Planning with Purpose:
Why Vision Still Matters   xv

PART I — THE GODLY VISION FOR YOUR LIFE

Chapter 1 — The Power of Vision   1
Chapter 2 — What Is a God-Given Vision?   7
Chapter 3 — Vision vs. Goals: Understanding Divine Foresight and Practical Targets   14
Chapter 4 — The Biblical Blueprint: Writing the Vision and Making It Plain   22
Chapter 5 — Preparing Your Life for Vision: Stewardship, Alignment, and Faith   29
Chapter 6 — Prophetic Goal Setting Prompts: Hearing and Responding to Heaven's Strategy   36
Chapter 7 — Declarations of Faith: Speaking Heaven's Blueprint Over Your Life   44
Testimonies of Vision Fulfilled   52

PART II — TURNING VISION INTO PROPHETIC GOALS

Chapter 8 — The Power of Godly Goals: Bridging Faith and Discipline   55
Chapter 9 — SMART Goals & Spirit-Led Guidance: Balancing Structure and Surrender   63
Chapter 10 — Categories and Timing: Understanding Divine Seasons and Goal Alignment   71
Chapter 11 — Prophetic Goal-Setting Prompts: Spirit-Led Structure for Action   78
Chapter 12 — Prayer Points for Divine Direction: Covering Your Goals in Intercession   87
Chapter 13 — Living in the Overflow: Maintaining Consistency, Gratitude, and Grace   95

PART III — WALKING IN DIVINE ALIGNMENT

Chapter 14 — Walking in Alignment Daily: Living as a Visionary Believer — 104
Chapter 15 — The Rewards of Alignment: Peace, Purpose, and Prophetic Power — 112
Chapter 16 — Finishing Strong: Enduring Faith and the Legacy of Vision — 118

Appendix A — Vision & Goal Setting Worksheets — 133
Appendix B — Prophetic Goal-Setting Templates — 148
Appendix C — Prophetic Declarations for Vision & Purpose — 149
Appendix D — Prophetic Goal Setting Checklists — 150
Appendix E — Prophetic Prompt Journal Pages — 151
Appendix F — Yearly & Quarterly Planning Pages — 156
Appendix G — Spiritual Warfare & Breakthrough Tools — 160
Endnotes (Scripture by Chapter) — 162
Bibliography — 166
Other Books by the Author — 167
About the Author — 168
Call to Action — 169
Call to Salvation and Deliverance — 172
Index — 175

Introduction

Every believer reaches a moment when desire alone is no longer enough. We want transformation, but transformation requires direction. We want change, but change requires clarity. We want fulfillment, but fulfillment requires alignment. Deep down, we know God has called us to more—but many of us don't know how to move from sensing purpose to actually living it.

For years, I have watched believers receive powerful prophetic words, stirring visions, and divine confirmations, only to struggle when it comes to walking them out. Not because they lacked faith, but because they lacked strategy, structure, and understanding. Prophecy reveals God's intention. But intention still requires participation.

That is where *Prophetic Goal Setting* enters the picture.

This book is not simply a manual about creating goals. It is an invitation to partner with God at a deeper level— where hearing meets doing, where vision meets movement, and where revelation matures into manifestation. This process is not about forcing plans but about aligning with Heaven's design for your life.

Prophetic goal setting teaches you how to:

- Recognize vision when God reveals it
- Distinguish between divine direction and personal desire
- Write the vision plainly and clearly

- Build Spirit-led goals that honor God's timing
- Pray strategically over your steps
- Maintain focus and consistency
- Walk daily in alignment with God's plan

You will be stretched. You will be challenged. You will be encouraged. And most importantly, you will be transformed—not by the strength of your willpower, but by the clarity that comes when the Holy Spirit illuminates your path.

This book is built on the truth that vision is not a suggestion—it is an assignment.
Purpose is not accidental—it is intentional.
Your destiny is not a mystery—it is a revelation waiting to be embraced.

As you begin this journey, open your heart. Expect God to speak. Expect clarity to rise. Expect old patterns to break. Expect new structure to form. And expect to step into the version of yourself that Heaven has already seen.

Welcome to a new level of alignment.
Welcome to divine focus.
Welcome to prophetic strategy and supernatural execution.

Welcome to *Prophetic Goal Setting: Aligning Your Vision with God's Plan*.

PART I:
The Godly Vision for Your Life

CHAPTER 1
The Power of Vision

"Where there is no vision, the people perish: but he that keepeth the law, happy is he." — **Proverbs 29:18 (KJV)**

Every great journey begins with a glimpse — not of the road ahead, but of the *destination*. Vision is that glimpse. It is the divine picture God allows you to see before you arrive. It is His way of revealing the end from the beginning, so that you may walk with purpose rather than drift through life without direction.

The truth is simple:

If you fail to plan, you plan to fail.

Those words, though often quoted in business circles, are deeply spiritual. Our Creator Himself is a planner — a God of structure, order, and purpose. Before He spoke light into being, He had already seen creation in its fullness. He envisioned it. Likewise, before you can build the life He intends, you must first see it in your spirit.

Albert Einstein once said,

"Paper is used to write things down that we need to remember; our brains are used to think."

Vision writing is not a business exercise — it's a sacred act of remembering what Heaven showed you. When you put God's revelation to paper, you are recording prophecy.

Why Vision Matters

Vision is not a luxury for the gifted few; it's a spiritual necessity for every believer. Without vision, we wander. With vision, we walk with divine precision.

The prophet Habakkuk understood this when he wrote:

"I will stand upon my watch, and set me upon the tower, and will watch to see what he will say unto me... And the Lord answered me, and said, Write the vision, and make it plain upon tables, that he may run that readeth it." — **Habakkuk 2:1–2**

Habakkuk was not told to simply *dream*; he was instructed to *write*. Writing transforms revelation into responsibility. The act of writing your vision signals to Heaven that you are ready to steward what God is showing you.

When God gives you a vision, it's not a suggestion — it's a summons. It calls you out of comfort and into destiny. It gives your faith an address, your prayers a purpose, and your actions a direction.

What Is Vision?

In Scripture, the Hebrew word for *vision* is **chāzôn** or **ḥāzôn (khaw-zone')** — meaning *prophecy, divine communication, revelation, or dream.* Vision is not just imagination; it is divine insight. It is a message from

Heaven to Earth, designed to align your natural life with God's supernatural blueprint.

To *see* in the Spirit is to receive a picture of something that does not yet exist naturally — but already exists in God's mind. Vision bridges the gap between what *is* and what *will be*.

Some visions come in flashes — a word during prayer, a dream, or an inner knowing. Others unfold slowly, shaped by time and obedience. Whether large or small, every true vision carries the same purpose: to pull you toward the person God designed you to become.

Characteristics of a God-Given Vision

1. **It aligns with divine purpose.**
   A Godly vision never contradicts His Word. It draws you closer to His will, not away from it.

2. **It inspires transformation.**
   When God shows you your future, it won't flatter your comfort — it will challenge your growth. A true vision will stretch your faith.

3. **It transcends your present reality.**
   Vision doesn't need to be realistic. Noah had never seen rain, yet built an ark. Abraham had no heir, yet saw generations. Faith doesn't consult statistics.

4. **It lasts beyond you.**
   A God vision endures through eternity. It's not about temporary success but eternal impact.

Seeing Before Doing

Before action comes vision. Many believers attempt to *do* without first learning to *see*. Yet Scripture is clear — even Jesus did only what He *saw* the Father doing (**John 5:19**). Vision gives your actions authority.

Without it, your energy disperses in many directions but yields little fruit. This is why prophetic goal setting begins not with a to-do list, but with time in God's presence. The Spirit of God reveals strategy to those who watch, wait, and listen. Like Habakkuk, you must first *stand upon your watch*.

Your secret place is your watchtower. It's where you gain divine perspective above the noise of daily life. From there, the Holy Spirit will begin to unveil images, ideas, or instructions that become your vision.

When Vision Feels Delayed

Habakkuk 2:3 reminds us, *"For the vision is yet for an appointed time… though it tarry, wait for it."* Vision carries timing. God may show you something now that won't manifest for years. That doesn't mean the vision is dead; it means it's *maturing*.

Seeds must remain buried before they bloom. Vision is like that seed — hidden, but alive. Waiting seasons are not wasted seasons; they are refining seasons. In the delay, God develops your character to match your calling.

Reflection: Aligning with Heaven's Blueprint

1. What has God shown you about your future that you've been too afraid to write down?

_____

_____

_____

_____

2. Have you confused *goals* (what you can achieve) with *vision* (what God has revealed)?

_____

_____

_____

_____

3. Where might impatience or fear be clouding your spiritual sight?

_____

_____

_____

_____

- Take a few quiet moments today to pray and listen.
- Ask the Holy Spirit to reveal or reaffirm His vision for your life.
- Write what you hear, even if it feels impossible.
- Remember: the point is not realism, but revelation.

Prophetic Declaration

- Father, thank You for the divine vision You've placed within me.
- I will no longer doubt what You've shown me. I receive clarity, courage, and conviction to see as You see.
- Though the vision may tarry, I will wait in faith, knowing that it will surely come to pass.
- My eyes are open, my heart is aligned, and my spirit is ready to walk in purpose.
- In Jesus' name, Amen.

CHAPTER 2
What Is a God-Given Vision?

"And it shall come to pass afterward, that I will pour out my Spirit upon all flesh; and your sons and your daughters shall prophesy, your old men shall dream dreams, your young men shall see visions." — **Joel 2:28 (KJV)**

Every believer has access to vision — not because of personal greatness, but because of divine grace. Vision is the language of the Spirit. It is how God reveals His intentions to His children, giving them a glimpse of His plans before those plans manifest on earth.

But how do we know when a vision is truly *from God*? How do we discern between divine revelation and human imagination? Understanding this distinction is foundational to prophetic goal setting.

Vision: Heaven's Communication Channel

In the Bible, the word *vision* is translated from the Hebrew **cḥāzôn** or **ḥāzôn** (pronounced *khaw-zone'*), which means *a divine revelation, prophecy, dream, or inspired insight*. This word is not passive—it implies a supernatural encounter that brings direction or correction.

A God-given vision is not just a good idea. It's not wishful thinking or ambition dressed in religious language. It is a *spiritual transmission*—a message from the mind of God to your spirit, designed to position you in alignment with His purpose.

When the prophets received visions, they weren't brainstorming their futures; they were *receiving heaven's instructions*. In the same way, when God grants you a vision, He's revealing your unique role in His grand design. Vision gives meaning to your journey and reveals why you were born for such a time as this.

Human Vision vs. Divine Vision

Not all visions are equal. Human vision comes from desire; divine vision comes from destiny.

Here's the difference:

Human Vision	God-Given Vision
Rooted in ambition	Rooted in revelation
Driven by personal success	Driven by kingdom purpose
Limited by resources	Fueled by faith
Focused on outcomes	Focused on obedience
Changes with emotions or trends	Anchored in eternal truth

This distinction is critical. Many people chase goals born of good intentions, but not divine instruction. Human vision may produce results, but only divine vision produces *fruit that remains.* (**John 15:16**)

The true test of a God-given vision is that it glorifies Him, not you. It stretches your faith but strengthens your dependence. It feels bigger than your capacity — and that's how you know it's from Heaven.

The Birthplace of Vision

Vision is conceived in *communion* with God. It is not discovered through striving, but through stillness. The Holy Spirit reveals vision to those who wait, watch, and listen.

Habakkuk modeled this posture:
"I will stand upon my watch, and set me upon the tower, and will watch to see what He will say unto me…"(**Habakkuk 2:1**)

Before God spoke, Habakkuk positioned himself. Vision begins not with noise, but with *watchfulness*. You can't receive revelation while constantly distracted by comparison, busyness, or fear.

The watchtower represents your place of prayer, intimacy, and attentiveness. When you consistently dwell there, your spiritual senses sharpen, and Heaven's messages become clear.

How God Communicates Vision

God speaks in diverse ways — and He knows exactly how to reach you. Vision may come through:

1. **Scripture** — A verse that ignites your spirit and reveals direction.

2. **Dreams or Spiritual Impressions** — A recurring image or idea that resonates deeply with your calling.

3. **Prophetic Words** — A confirmation spoken through another believer.

4. **Inner Conviction** — A holy restlessness or peace guiding you toward a particular purpose.

5. **Circumstantial Alignment** — Open or closed doors that make His will undeniable.

Whatever the channel, the purpose remains the same: God gives vision to guide His people toward destiny.

But remember not every open door is divine, and not every delay is demonic. Vision requires discernment — a heart attuned to both Scripture and the Spirit.

The Nature of Divine Vision

1. **It Calls You Higher**
   A God vision doesn't cater to your comfort zone. It challenges you to grow spiritually, mentally, and emotionally. It invites transformation before manifestation.

2. **It Requires Faith**
   Hebrews 11:1 says, *"Faith is the substance of things hoped for, the evidence of things not seen."* Vision and faith are inseparable; one shows you the

destination, the other empowers you to journey toward it.

3. **It Unfolds Over Time**
   God rarely reveals the full picture at once. Vision often comes in stages — a glimpse here, a confirmation there. Each act of obedience reveals the next step.

4. **It Serves Others**
   True vision never ends with you. God's revelation always contributes to the blessing, healing, or advancement of others. If it's only about personal gain, it's not a Kingdom vision.

Guarding the Vision

Once you receive divine vision, protect it. The enemy's goal is not to take your salvation — it's to blind your sight. If he can keep you visionless, he can keep you powerless.

Guard your vision by:

- **Writing it down.** What you don't record, you may forget.

- **Praying over it regularly.** Intercession keeps it alive in your spirit.

- **Sharing it wisely.** Not everyone deserves access to what God whispered in secret.

- **Refining it through Scripture.** The Word of God keeps your vision pure and aligned.

Remember Joseph. When he shared his God-given dreams prematurely, his brothers hated him for it **(Genesis 37)**. Not everyone can interpret your dream correctly — some will mock it; others will misunderstand it. Protect your revelation until God gives the release to reveal.

Reflection: Hearing and Seeing in the Spirit

1. How do you currently discern when God is speaking versus when you're following personal ambition?

   _____

   _____

   _____

   _____

2. What distractions or fears might be blocking your ability to *see* clearly?

   _____

   _____

   _____

   _____

3. Have you written down your vision, or is it still only in your thoughts?

_____

_____

_____

_____

- Spend a few quiet minutes meditating on **Habakkuk 2:1–3**.
- Ask the Holy Spirit to rekindle any vision that has grown dim or forgotten. He is faithful to remind you of what He first revealed.

Prophetic Declaration

- Lord, open the eyes of my understanding to see what You are revealing.
- I choose to silence every voice that contradicts Your Word.
- I receive divine sight and clarity of purpose.
- My vision will not be hijacked by fear, pride, or distraction.
- I will watch and wait until You speak.
- I will write what You show me and walk it out in obedience.
- In Jesus' name, Amen.

CHAPTER 3
Vision vs. Goals
Understanding Divine Foresight & Practical Targets

"For I know the thoughts that I think toward you, saith the Lord, thoughts of peace, and not of evil, to give you an expected end." — **Jeremiah 29:11 (KJV)**

Every believer longs to walk in God's plan, but many confuse the destination with the directions. Vision is the destination; goals are the directions. Vision reveals where you are going, while goals define how you will get there.

Both are essential — but they are not the same. When you understand the difference, you stop striving in the flesh and start walking in divine alignment.

The Heavenly Blueprint vs. The Human Blueprint

Vision originates from divine foresight — God revealing a glimpse of His plan for your life. It's the *why* behind your purpose. Goals, however, are the *how* — the practical, step-by-step targets that bring the vision into tangible form.

Without vision, your goals have no anchor. Without goals, your vision has no movement.

Vision inspires. Goals implement.

Think of it like building a house. The vision is the architect's design — the final picture of the home. The goals are the construction steps — laying the foundation, raising the walls, installing the roof.

Without the design, the work lacks direction. Without the work, the design remains only a dream.

Vision: The Big Picture

Vision answers the question,

"What is God calling me to become or accomplish?"

It's the long-term divine picture of your future — often something far greater than your current ability or resources.

God's visions are eternal. They outlast your season and sometimes even your lifetime. Abraham's vision of being a father of nations didn't end with Isaac; it continued through generations.

A true vision from God will always:

- Stretch your faith beyond your logic.

- Align with Scripture and Kingdom principles.

- Point back to God's glory, not personal achievement.

Vision requires belief before evidence. It's seeing through spiritual eyes what has not yet appeared in the natural.

Goals: The Steps Toward Fulfillment

Goals answer the question,

"What must I do today to move toward the vision God has given me?"

They are practical, measurable, and time-bound actions that give structure to your faith.

In the natural, goals may appear mundane — waking earlier, saving money, studying a new skill, finishing a degree — but spiritually, each one is an act of *obedience*. Every step you take toward a divine vision is a declaration that you trust God's plan enough to act on it.

Joshua 1:8 reminds us:

"This book of the law shall not depart out of thy mouth; but thou shalt meditate therein day and night... then thou shalt make thy way prosperous, and then thou shalt have good success."

Success, in God's economy, is not luck — it's obedience to divine instruction. Setting and pursuing goals is one way we cooperate with God's plan.

Comparing Vision and Goals

Vision	Goals
Reveals the *destination*	Provides the *directions*
Comes from divine revelation	Comes from deliberate planning
Limitless and eternal	Specific and time-bound
Requires faith	Requires discipline
Speaks to your purpose	Shapes your daily priorities
May seem impossible	Makes the impossible achievable one step at a time

When Vision and Goals Work Together

When vision and goals unite, something powerful happens — *faith meets focus.*

Faith without works is dead (**James 2:17**), but works without vision are meaningless. You need both. Vision gives your spirit wings; goals give those wings flight paths. Vision speaks to the *why*; goals execute the *how*.

Imagine a person who has a beautiful God-given vision of building a ministry to serve youth but never sets practical steps — recruiting volunteers, finding a venue, or fundraising. The vision remains suspended in the realm of potential. Conversely, a person who sets many goals but lacks a divine vision may achieve success yet feel unfulfilled, because their achievements lack eternal purpose.

Divine foresight paired with practical targets brings harmony between heaven and earth — revelation and responsibility working as one.

Common Mistakes in Balancing Vision and Goals

1. **Mistaking activity for progress**
   Doing more doesn't always mean you're moving in the right direction. Without vision, activity becomes distraction.

2. **Setting goals without prayer**
   Goals birthed from self-will may succeed temporarily but will drain you spiritually. Seek God's counsel before you commit your plans.

3. **Waiting for perfection before acting**
   Vision unfolds as you move. Abraham didn't know the whole journey — he simply obeyed the first instruction.

4. **Ignoring God's timing**
   Goals must honor divine timing. You can't force a harvest in the wrong season. When the Holy Spirit says, "Wait," waiting is an act of faith.

Allowing God to Override Your Plans

In my teaching on *Prophetic Goal Setting – Part II*, I emphasized that God may give goals that are not "S.M.A.R.T" by human standards. This truth is crucial. The acronym *S.M.A.R.T.* (Specific, Measurable,

Achievable, Relevant, Time-bound) is valuable — but it must remain Spirit-led.

God's instructions sometimes defy logic.
He told Noah to build an ark before rain existed.
He told Gideon to reduce his army before battle.
He told Peter to walk on water.
None of these were "achievable" by human reasoning — yet each fulfilled divine vision perfectly.

Proverbs 16:9 reminds us:
"A man's heart deviseth his way: but the Lord directeth his steps."

Make your plans — but surrender them daily. The highest form of planning is *yielded obedience*.

Reflection: Aligning Your Foresight and Focus

1. What has God shown you that still feels "too big" for you to pursue?

   _____

   _____

   _____

   _____

2. Have your daily goals reflected your long-term divine vision, or have you been distracted by lesser pursuits?

3. What would it look like for you to surrender your to-do list to the Holy Spirit and ask Him to edit it?

- Spend time journaling what God has revealed and what practical steps you sense He's asking you to take.
- Then, commit them in prayer.

Prophetic Declaration

- Father, thank You for the vision You've entrusted to me.
- I receive divine wisdom to translate heavenly revelation into earthly action.
- My goals will align with Your will, and my steps will follow Your Spirit.

- Where I have been distracted, bring me back into focus.
- I will not confuse busyness with progress, nor ambition with calling.
- I will dream boldly, plan wisely, and act faithfully.
- In Jesus' name, Amen.

CHAPTER 4
The Biblical Blueprint
Writing the Vision & Making It Plain

"And the Lord answered me, and said, Write the vision, and make it plain upon tables, that he may run that readeth it. For the vision is yet for an appointed time, but at the end it shall speak, and not lie: though it tarry, wait for it; because it will surely come, it will not tarry." — **Habakkuk 2:2–3 (KJV)**

Habakkuk's Posture

Before we can discuss the *act* of writing the vision, we must understand the *posture* that precedes it.

Habakkuk didn't receive the vision while running or reacting — he received it while *watching*. Verse 1 says, *"I will stand upon my watch, and set me upon the tower, and will watch to see what He will say unto me."*

This is the first blueprint:

Vision begins with stillness.

In a world filled with constant noise and endless movement, it's easy to miss the voice of God because we are too busy trying to create our own momentum. But the Kingdom does not operate on human urgency — it operates on divine timing. The prophetic believer learns to slow down long enough to *see what God is saying.*

Sometimes, Heaven's strategy comes not in a shout, but in a whisper.

If you want to receive the blueprint, you must first be willing to wait on the Architect.

Step One: Write the Vision

When God told Habakkuk to *write* the vision, it wasn't for decoration or documentation — it was for activation.

Writing the vision is an act of faith. It transfers what God has revealed from the unseen realm into the tangible world. It also becomes a record of accountability — something you can revisit, pray over, and build upon.

In ancient times, scribes wrote on *tablets* — clay or stone surfaces that preserved important words. God's instruction to "make it plain upon tables" implies that what He reveals to you must be both *visible* and *clear*. It's not enough to keep your vision locked in your memory; it must be inscribed where you can *see it, speak it, and steward it.*

Faith written becomes focus.

When you write your vision:

1. **You clarify what you believe.**
   Writing exposes vague ideas and forces precision.

2. **You anchor your faith.**
   The written word serves as a reminder during seasons of doubt.

3. **You create a legacy.**
   A written vision can outlive you — influencing others long after you've moved on.

Step Two: Make It Plain

Clarity is a spiritual principle.

Many believers hear from God but never interpret His instructions clearly enough to follow them.
"Make it plain" means to express the vision in a way that is understandable, actionable, and repeatable.

God doesn't give confusing directions — but we often complicate His simplicity. Your written vision doesn't need lofty language; it needs clarity.

Ask yourself:

- Can I explain this vision to a child and have them understand it?

- Can I summarize it in one sentence?
- Does this vision align with Scripture and the character of Christ?

If the answer to these questions is yes, you are writing the vision the way Heaven intended.

Step Three: Run With It

The verse continues: *"...that he may run that readeth it."* The written vision is not just for reflection — it's for motion. Once your vision is written, it becomes a map. It gives direction to your energy, clarity to your actions, and unity to your decisions.

To "run" doesn't mean to rush; it means to move with momentum and purpose. A clear vision empowers you to make faster, Spirit-led decisions.

You stop second-guessing every opportunity because you can now discern whether something aligns with your assignment.

> **When the vision is clear, confusion loses its power.**

Step Four: Trust God's Timing

Habakkuk 2:3 gives a crucial reminder: *"For the vision is yet for an appointed time..."*

Every God-given vision has a divine schedule. You can't manipulate the clock of Heaven, but you can prepare for its fulfillment.

The word *appointed* in Hebrew (*moed*) refers to a divinely designated season — a moment pre-marked by God. This means your vision is not delayed; it's developing.

Like a seed planted in the soil, it is growing even when unseen. Your role is not to force it but to nurture it — through prayer, obedience, and patience.

Biblical Examples of Written Vision

1. **Moses and the Tablets (Exodus 31:18)**
   God Himself wrote the Ten Commandments on stone. He valued permanence and clarity.

2. **John and Revelation (Revelation 1:11)**
   "Write on a scroll what you see…" The vision given to John became a book that continues to instruct generations.

3. **Nehemiah's Plan (Nehemiah 2)**
   Before rebuilding Jerusalem's walls, Nehemiah documented a strategy — a written plan that led to success in record time.

Each example shows the same pattern: revelation, writing, and then realization.

Vision Writing Exercise

- Set aside 30 quiet minutes this week.
- Find a notebook or journal you will dedicate solely to your prophetic vision journey.

1. Begin with Worship.
Invite the Holy Spirit to bring to remembrance everything He has whispered over your life — dreams, prophecies, or recurring themes.

2. **Ask Yourself:**
   - What has God placed in my heart that refuses to die?
   - What burden or passion keeps resurfacing?
   - If nothing were impossible, what would I build, serve, or create for His glory?

3. **Write Freely.**
Don't overthink grammar or structure. Let revelation flow before refinement. You can organize later — right now, capture what Heaven is saying.

4. **Review and Simplify.**
After writing, read through your words. Highlight recurring phrases or images. These often reveal your *core vision statement*. Reduce your vision into one to three clear sentences that summarize your calling.
Example: *"To equip believers to hear God's voice clearly and walk in prophetic purpose."*

5. **Pray Over It.**
Seal your writing in prayer. Speak it aloud daily. Let your words agree with Heaven.

Reflection: The Blueprint Within

1. Have you written your vision clearly enough that someone else could "run with it"?

   _____

   _____

   _____

2. What part of your vision feels delayed — and could that delay be God's appointed timing?

_____

_____

_____

_____

3. How can you keep your written vision visible and active in your daily life? (e.g., vision board, journal, wall art)

_____

_____

_____

_____

Prophetic Declaration

- Lord, thank You for entrusting me with vision.
- Today, I commit to write what You have shown me and make it plain.
- I will no longer keep divine revelation buried in my thoughts — I will give it voice and form.
- Though the vision may tarry, I will wait in faith and work in obedience.

- Let every word You've spoken over my life come to pass in its appointed time.
- In Jesus' name, Amen.

CHAPTER 5
Preparing Your Life for Vision
Stewardship, Alignment, & Faith

"But thou shalt remember the Lord thy God: for it is He that giveth thee power to get wealth, that He may establish His covenant..." — **Deuteronomy 8:18**

Vision may begin in revelation, but it is sustained through preparation.

When God entrusts you with a divine assignment, He expects you to prepare your life to carry it. A vision from Heaven requires a vessel on Earth that can sustain it with character, consistency, and faith.

You can't expect Heaven to release what your life can't yet hold.

Preparation is not punishment—it's proof that you are serious about your purpose.

Stewardship — Caring for What You Already Have

Many believers pray for greater vision while neglecting the resources already in their hands. Yet Jesus said,

"He that is faithful in that which is least is faithful also in much." — **Luke 16:10**

Before God entrusts you with nations, He watches how you manage your neighborhood. Before He releases the next level, He observes your faithfulness in the current one.

Practical Stewardship Checklist:

☐ **Time:** Do you treat your hours as sacred currency or as something to spend casually?

☐ **Finances:** Do you handle your money with integrity and generosity?

☐ **Relationships:** Are you nurturing divine connections and walking in forgiveness?

☐ **Talents:** Are your gifts sitting dormant or being developed for God's glory?

Faithful stewardship turns potential into promotion. When God sees that you value what He's already given, He expands your capacity for more.

Preparation proves trustworthiness.

Alignment — Positioning for Purpose

The next step in preparing for vision is alignment.

You may have a clear vision, but if your life isn't positioned with God's order, the vision will struggle to manifest. Alignment simply means *living in harmony with Heaven's design.*

Three Areas of Alignment

1. **Spiritual Alignment**
   Keep your relationship with God first. Everything flows from intimacy with Him. Prayer, Word meditation, fasting, and worship are not spiritual chores—they are fuel for clarity.

2. **Relational Alignment**
   The right people accelerate your purpose; the wrong ones drain it. Abraham couldn't walk fully in his calling until he separated from Lot (**Genesis 13:14**). Ask the Holy Spirit to reveal which relationships are seasonal and which are covenantal.

3. **Mental Alignment**
   Romans 12:2 urges us to be transformed by the renewing of our minds. You cannot carry a prophetic vision with a pessimistic mindset. Shift your internal narrative to match Heaven's perspective: *I can do all things through Christ who strengthens me.*

When your spirit, relationships, and mind align with God, the atmosphere around you begins to cooperate with your assignment.

Faith — Believing Before Seeing

Vision always requires faith because God shows you the *end* before the *beginning*.

Faith bridges that gap. **Hebrews 11:8** says, *"By faith Abraham, when he was called to go out… obeyed; and he went out, not knowing whither he went."*

Faith is not blind optimism—it is trust in God's character when the outcome is still invisible.

When you prepare by faith:
- You obey before understanding.
- You praise before results.
- You invest in what hasn't yet appeared.

Faith turns your preparation into prophecy in motion. Each small act—writing a plan, taking a class, saving money, mentoring others—signals to Heaven that you believe what God said.

Purity of Motives

Preparation also includes refining your *why*.

Ask yourself: *Why do I want this vision to come to pass?* If ambition or comparison drives you, pause and let the Holy Spirit purify your motives. God blesses vision that flows from love, not ego.

Psalm 24:4–5 describes those who ascend the hill of the

Lord as having *clean hands and a pure heart*. Purity invites provision.

Practical Preparation Steps

1. **Create a Sacred Space** – Dedicate a room, desk, or corner where you pray, write, and plan with God.

2. **Establish Rhythms of Rest** – Vision requires energy; burnout blurs hearing. Rest is spiritual obedience.

3. **Educate Yourself** – Study, read, and seek mentorship related to your assignment. Faith grows when fed by wisdom.

4. **Organize Your Environment** – Order in your surroundings often brings order in your spirit.

5. **Serve Faithfully Where You Are** – Service refines humility. God often promotes servants before dreamers.

Preparation is the soil where prophetic seeds take root.

Reflection — Preparing the Ground

1. What area of your life feels unprepared for the weight of your vision—time, finances, mindset, or relationships?

_____

_____

_____

_____

2. Which practical step can you take this week to demonstrate stewardship?

_____

_____

_____

_____

3. How can you realign your daily habits with God's priorities?

_____

_____

_____

_____

Write your answers in your vision journal, and invite the Holy Spirit to highlight one specific area to begin cultivating.

Prophetic Declaration

- Father, I thank You for trusting me with vision.
- Today I choose to prepare my life as fertile ground for Your purpose.
- I will steward well what I already have, align my heart with Your Word, and walk by faith even when the path is unclear.
- Purify my motives and strengthen my discipline.
- As I prepare, let Heaven prepare the way before me.
- In Jesus' name, Amen.

CHAPTER 6
Prophetic Goal Setting Prompts
Hearing and Responding to Heaven's Strategy

"The plans of the diligent lead only to abundance; but all who rush in arrive only at want." — **Proverbs 21:5 (CJB)**

A prophetic life is not accidental—it is intentional. God gives vision, but He also provides *strategy*.

Prophetic goal setting is the bridge between hearing God's promise and walking in its fulfillment.

When you plan prophetically, you're not trying to control outcomes; you're learning to cooperate with Heaven's design. It's less about scheduling and more about synchronizing—moving in rhythm with God's timing, God's wisdom, and God's leading.

The Balance Between Faith and Foresight

Faith does not cancel planning.

Planning, when done in partnership with the Holy Spirit, becomes an act of faith. You are declaring:

> **I believe God will do what He said, and I am preparing to receive it.**

Joseph in Egypt didn't just interpret Pharaoh's dream—he also created a plan. He stored grain during seven years of plenty so that Egypt would survive seven years of famine. His prophetic insight produced a practical strategy, and that combination preserved nations.

You, too, are called to plan prophetically listening for God's voice as you design steps that position your life for fruitfulness.

What Is Prophetic Goal Setting?

Prophetic goal setting is the Spirit-led process of writing actionable steps in response to divine revelation.

It involves:
1. Listening for divine instruction.
2. Recording what you hear.
3. Discerning the right time and order for execution.
4. Aligning each plan with Scripture and Kingdom purpose.

Prophetic goal setting is not about guessing the future; it's about preparing for what God has already revealed.

Seven Prophetic Prompts

- Use the following prompts as guided exercises.
- Set aside quiet, undistracted time for each one.
- Read a short passage of Scripture, then pause to write what you sense the Lord saying.
- Don't rush; let revelation flow through reflection and prayer.

Prophetic Prompt #1 — What Has God Already Said?

"Man shall not live by bread alone, but by every word that proceeds from the mouth of God." — **Matthew 4:4**

Before you ask for new direction, revisit what God has already spoken.

Write down past prophecies, dreams, or scriptures that have repeatedly stirred your heart.

Ask the Holy Spirit:
- *Which of these words still applies to my current season?*
- *Have I obeyed the last instruction You gave me?*

God rarely gives new revelation to those who have ignored the previous one.

Prophetic Prompt #2 — What Season Am I In?

"To everything there is a season, and a time to every purpose under heaven." — **Ecclesiastes 3:1**

Discern your season. Are you in preparation, building, waiting, or harvest? Each season demands a different type of planning.

Ask:
- *What fruit is God developing in me right now?*
- *What actions would be premature in this season?*

When you identify your season, you learn to pace yourself according to Heaven's rhythm.

Prophetic Prompt #3 — What Resources Has God Placed Around Me?

"What is that in your hand?" — **Exodus 4:2**

Moses already had a staff—God just revealed its supernatural potential.

Look around you: what gifts, connections, or tools are already within reach?
List your current resources.

Then, ask:
- *How can I use what I already have to take one step toward my vision?*

Prophetic wisdom multiplies what exists rather than waiting for what's missing.

Prophetic Prompt #4 — Who Am I Called to Serve?

"The greatest among you will be your servant." — **Matthew 23:11**

Every vision has an audience. You are not called to everyone, but you are called to *someone*.

Ask:
- *Who benefits when I walk in obedience?*
- *Whose needs does my calling meet?*

Defining your "who" brings focus to your "why." God expands your reach when your motive is service.

Prophetic Prompt #5 — What Obstacles Must I Confront?

"Every valley shall be exalted, and every mountain and hill shall be made low." — **Isaiah 40:4**

Prophetic goal setting includes honest confrontation.

List the internal and external barriers between you and your next step—fear, procrastination, disorganization, lack of faith, or unhealthy partnerships.
Pray over each obstacle.

Then ask:
- *What action can I take this week to remove or reduce this barrier?*

Vision thrives in clarity; fear thrives in avoidance.
Address the obstacles prophetically and practically.

Prophetic Prompt #6 — What Does Obedience Look Like Right Now?

"Whatever He says to you, do it." — **John 2:5**

Sometimes prophetic instruction is simple: *call this person, write that email, start that course, sow that seed.*

Write down one clear, immediate act of obedience that aligns with your vision.
Then do it promptly.
Delay dulls discernment; obedience sharpens it.

Prophetic Prompt #7 — What Is Heaven's Timeline?

"At the end it shall speak, and not lie: though it tarry, wait for it; because it will surely come." — **Habakkuk 2:3**

Ask God for timing. Not every door opens immediately, and not every delay is denial.

In your journal, create a simple timeline or calendar, asking:
- *What can I begin now?*
- *What needs more preparation?*
- *What requires waiting on divine alignment?*

Record what you sense the Holy Spirit emphasizing. The goal isn't to predict dates—it's to perceive seasons.

Turning Prompts into Plans

Once you've completed all seven prompts, review your notes prayerfully. Highlight recurring themes, scriptures, or ideas. These are clues to your next steps. Then, translate what you've heard into actionable faith goals.

For example:

- *Vision:* Empower women to live prophetically.

- *Prophetic Prompt Result:* Start small groups in your community.

- *Action Plan:* Host one online prayer meeting this quarter and build from there.

The more you write, the clearer your path becomes. Remember: clarity is cumulative—it grows as you walk.

Reflection — Listening for Strategy

1. Which prompt revealed the most insight or conviction?

   _____

   _____

   _____

   _____

2. Did any instruction surprise you or confirm something you already sensed?

   _____

   _____

   _____

   _____

3. What small step can you take this week to begin aligning with Heaven's strategy?

   _____

___

___

___

Prophetic Declaration

- Lord, thank You for being the Master Planner of my life.
- I open my ears to hear and my heart to obey.
- Reveal Heaven's strategy for this season.
- I will not rush ahead of You, nor lag behind.
- Teach me to plan prophetically—to prepare, position, and act with wisdom.
- Every plan I write will align with Your perfect will and bear lasting fruit.
- In Jesus' name, Amen.

CHAPTER 7
Declarations of Faith
Speaking Heaven's Blueprint Over Your Life

"Death and life are in the power of the tongue: and they that love it shall eat the fruit thereof." — **Proverbs 18:21 (KJV)**

When God gives you a vision, He expects you not only to *write it*, but also to *speak it*.

Your words are spiritual instruments — they build, shape, and call forth what Heaven has already ordained. Every declaration you make in faith partners with God's creative power to manifest His will in your life.

Heaven moves in response to agreement.

When you speak what God has said, you activate His blueprint on Earth.

Why Declarations Matter

Words are not casual in the Kingdom; they are creative. From Genesis 1, we learn that God *spoke* the universe into existence. Light appeared because He said, "Let there be light."

If you are made in His image, your words also carry creative authority.

Faith that remains silent is incomplete. When you open

your mouth in agreement with Heaven, you give sound to the unseen.

Declarations:

1. **Reinforce your faith** — reminding your spirit what God has promised.

2. **Shift your atmosphere** — aligning your environment with divine order.

3. **Defeat doubt** — silencing the voice of fear with the voice of truth.

4. **Direct your focus** — keeping your attention on God's promises instead of your problems.

Every declaration is a seed — and seeds grow into harvests when consistently sown.

Speaking What Heaven Has Already Written

When you speak the Word of God, you are not convincing Heaven to move — you are authorizing Earth to align.

Declarations are not begging prayers; they are faith statements rooted in divine revelation. For example:

- You don't say, *"I hope God provides."*
  You declare, *"My God shall supply all my needs according to His riches in glory."* (Philippians 4:19)

- You don't say, *"I might walk in purpose."*
  You declare, *"I was created for good works, prepared in advance for me to do."* (Ephesians 2:10)

You are not wishing—you are witnessing.
You're echoing Heaven's verdict until Earth complies.

Guidelines for Prophetic Declarations

1. **Base Them on Scripture**
   Every declaration should stand on the Word of God. His Word is your legal authority in the spirit.

2. **Speak in Present Tense**
   Declare as though it already is. You are agreeing with the eternal reality of Heaven, not the temporary facts of Earth.

3. **Be Consistent**
   Repetition reinforces reality. Daily declaration builds spiritual muscle.

4. **Add Emotion and Faith**
   Don't whisper your destiny—speak with conviction. Heaven responds to sincerity and belief.

5. **Combine with Action**
   Faith without works is dead. Let your behavior align with what your mouth proclaims.

Daily Declarations for Vision and Alignment

Here are sample declarations inspired by the principles throughout *Part I*.

Read them aloud daily, or adapt them to your personal vision statement.

Declarations of Identity

- I am a child of God, created with divine purpose and destiny.
- The Spirit of the Lord lives in me, giving me wisdom, strength, and clarity.

- I walk by faith, not by sight.

- My mind is renewed, my heart is steadfast, and my steps are ordered by the Lord.

Declarations of Vision

- I see clearly what God has shown me.

- My vision aligns with Heaven's blueprint.

- Though it tarries, I will wait in faith, for it will surely come to pass.

- I will write, speak, and act according to what the Spirit has revealed.

- My eyes are fixed on Jesus, the author and finisher of my faith.

Declarations of Stewardship

- I am faithful with what I have, and God is enlarging my capacity for more.

- I manage my time, talents, and treasure with integrity and excellence.

- I am a wise steward of divine resources.

- My diligence leads to abundance, and my preparation attracts promotion.

Declarations of Provision and Overflow

- I will live the *Zoe* life—the God-kind of life—in peace, health, and prosperity.

- I have the power to get wealth that I may establish God's covenant on Earth.

- Heaven's resources are open over me; I live in divine supply.

- I am a cheerful giver and a faithful tither.

- I live in the overflow, not in lack.

Declarations of Obedience and Focus

- I hear the voice of the Holy Spirit clearly and follow His instructions promptly.

- I will not rush ahead of God, nor shrink back in fear.

- My goals are aligned with His vision for my life.

- Every distraction loses power over me.

- I am steadfast, immovable, always abounding in the work of the Lord.

Declarations of Purpose and Legacy

- I was born for such a time as this.

- My life impacts generations for the glory of God.

- Everything I build will carry eternal value.

- My vision will outlive me and continue to bear fruit.

- I will finish my course with joy and fulfill my ministry.

Speaking Faith When It Feels Hard

Even when you don't feel it, speak it.

Declarations aren't rooted in emotion—they're rooted in truth.
When doubt whispers, answer with the Word. When fear speaks, respond with faith.

Your declaration isn't denial of reality; it's defiance of limitation.

You are not ignoring the facts—you're elevating your focus to the higher truth of God's promise.

> **You can't speak defeat and expect victory. You can't prophesy lack and expect abundance.**

Change your language, and you'll change your life.

Reflection — Your Voice and Vision

1. What words have you been speaking over your vision—faith or frustration?

   _____

   _____

   _____

   _____

2. Which declaration above resonates most deeply with your current season?

   _____

   _____

   _____

   _____

3. What new declaration do you feel led to write for yourself today?

_____

_____

_____

_____

Write your personalized declaration in your vision journal. Read it aloud every morning until it becomes part of your daily rhythm of faith.

Prophetic Declaration

- Father, I thank You for the power of words.
- I declare that my mouth is an instrument of faith, not fear.
- Every promise You have spoken over my life shall come to pass.
- My voice will echo Heaven's truth until it manifests on Earth.
- I will live, move, and speak according to Your divine vision for me.
- In Jesus' name, Amen.

Testimonies of Vision Fulfilled

As you prepare to move from receiving vision into executing godly goals, I want to share two powerful testimonies from individuals who applied prophetic planning with faith and obedience. These stories reveal what is possible when believers align with Heaven's instruction and steward vision with intentionality.

A Prophetic Drawing That Became a Building

One man in our ministry attended a Prophetic Goal Setting class and followed each instruction with sincerity. During a prayer exercise, the Holy Spirit showed him a massive building—one He revealed the man would one day own. He drew the building exactly as he saw it, not knowing how or when it would come to pass.

Two years later, that prophetic vision became reality. The building he purchased was an exact replica of the drawing he created in class.

He didn't have the funds at the time.
What he had was prayer and Godly counsel.
God gave him strategy, wisdom, and supernatural favor to leverage the deal.
What began as a divine picture became a manifested promise.

A Homeownership Breakthrough Written Into Being

In another class, a woman desired to buy a home. She wrote her plan during the Prophetic Goal Setting session, aligned it with Scripture, and committed the journey to prayer.

One year later, she stood as a homeowner.

The same vision she wrote down became the home she lived in.

Her testimony stands as a reminder that when God breathes on a plan, obedience and consistency open the way for miracles.

These testimonies are not coincidences.

They are evidence of what happens when believers see what God sees, write what God says, and walk in obedience.

Now that you've completed the vision portion, let these stories build your faith as you step into Part II — Executing Prophetic Goals.

PART II:
Turning Vision into Prophetic Goals

CHAPTER 8
The Power of Godly Goals
Bridging Faith and Discipline

"Commit to the Lord whatever you do, and He will establish your plans." — **Proverbs 16:3 (NIV)**

Godly goals are the pathway between divine revelation and earthly manifestation.

If vision is what God shows you, goals are what you choose to *do* with what He has shown you.

Every prophecy requires partnership. When God reveals His will, He is inviting you into co-labor with Him—faith on His side, obedience on yours. Goals are how faith becomes motion.

The Divine Rhythm of Vision and Goals

> **Vision without goals remains inspiration. Goals without vision become mere activity. But when vision and goals unite, purpose gains power.**

God is strategic. He doesn't only speak promises; He outlines processes. From the design of creation to the building of the ark, His order is evident: plan, prepare, execute, rest.

Even Jesus modeled this rhythm. In **John 5:19**, He said, *"The Son can do nothing by Himself; He can do only what He sees His Father doing."*

Jesus lived by divine vision—but He *acted* on that vision daily through specific, Spirit-led steps.
Godly goals are your way of doing the same.

Why Goals Matter in the Kingdom

Many believers shy away from goal setting because they fear it might be too "worldly" or self-focused. But in truth, planning is biblical stewardship.

Consider these examples:

- **Noah** received a vision of the flood—but he built the ark one plank at a time.

- **Joseph** saw years of famine—but he set up a national storage plan.

- **Nehemiah** dreamed of a rebuilt wall—but he assigned workers by section and timeline.

Each had divine vision, but it was *goals* that made the vision visible.

**Godly goals don't replace faith—
they organize it**.

What Makes a Goal "Godly"?

A *godly goal* is not merely a personal ambition with Christian language attached. It is a Spirit-directed commitment aligned with God's character, Word, and purpose for your life.

Four Marks of Godly Goals

1. **They Align with Scripture**
   No goal that violates biblical principles can carry divine blessing. Your aim must echo His truth.

2. **They Require Faith**
   If you can accomplish it without God, it's not a God-sized goal. Divine assignments stretch your limits.

3. **They Serve Others**
   Kingdom goals always carry compassion. They bless people, not just profiles.

4. **They Bring Glory to God**
   Your ultimate measure of success is not applause—it's obedience.

Faith and Discipline: The Dynamic Duo

Faith gives you confidence that God will do what He said.

Discipline proves you believe Him enough to act. Goals are where faith and discipline meet.

Faith dreams it.
Discipline builds it.

Joshua 1:8 reminds us that prosperity and "good success" come from meditating on and *doing* the Word. That "doing" includes organized, deliberate steps toward what God has revealed.

> **Faith gives you the courage to begin; discipline gives you the endurance to continue.**

The Enemy of Divine Progress: Vagueness

One of the greatest barriers to purpose is vagueness. You cannot aim at what you cannot define.

Many believers say things like, "I want to grow in ministry," or "I want to walk in my calling." Those are good desires—but without clarity, they lack traction. God is not vague. His instructions to Noah included measurements. His plan for Moses included tabernacle blueprints. When God reveals vision, He also invites you to articulate it.

Write your goals clearly. Specificity honors revelation.

The Spiritual Nature of Planning

Planning is not presumption—it's participation. When you make Spirit-led plans, you are saying, "Lord, I believe You enough to prepare."

Deuteronomy 8:18 says, *"It is He that gives you power to get wealth."* Power implies action—effort directed by divine enablement. God gives the power, but you must still plant the seed, manage the time, and make the decision.

Practical planning demonstrates prophetic maturity. It proves that you value Heaven's vision enough to steward it intentionally.

Faith Goals vs. Flesh Goals

Faith Goals	Flesh Goals
Birth from prayer and revelation	Birth from ego or competition
Depend on grace and obedience	Depend on willpower alone
Build the Kingdom	Build personal comfort
Glorify God through service	Glorify self through success
Bring peace and fruitfulness	Bring pressure and burnout

A "faith goal" is not always impressive by worldly standards. Sometimes, it's as simple as *"Wake up 30 minutes earlier for prayer,"* or *"Forgive that person."*

The size doesn't determine the impact—obedience does.

The Process of Setting Godly Goals

1. **Start with Prayer** — Ask the Holy Spirit to reveal where He wants you to focus.

2. **Clarify Your Vision** — Review your written vision from Part I and ask, *"What specific goals will help me walk this out?"*

3. **Write S.M.A.R.T Goals** — Specific, Measurable, Achievable, Relevant, Time-bound—but always *Spirit-led.*

4. **Review Regularly** — Keep your goals before the Lord. Evaluate progress with humility, not perfectionism.

5. **Celebrate Faithfulness, Not Just Results** — Heaven measures obedience, not output.

When God Adjusts the Plan

Even well-laid goals must remain flexible.

Sometimes, the Holy Spirit redirects your focus mid-journey.

Proverbs 16:9 reminds us:
"A man's heart plans his way, but the Lord directs his steps."

Don't cling to your goals more tightly than to God Himself. If He shifts your path, follow willingly. Remember—He's not canceling your vision; He's *calibrating* it.

Reflection — Faith in Motion

1. What current goals in your life feel purely human, and which feel truly Spirit-inspired?

_____

_____

_____

_____

2. How can you add faith or discipline to strengthen those goals?

_____

_____

_____

_____

3. In what area might God be asking you to simplify or surrender your plan?

_____

_____

_____

_____

Prophetic Declaration

- Father, I thank You for the power to plan with purpose.
- I will set goals that align with Your Word and advance Your Kingdom.
- My discipline is an act of worship; my diligence is an offering of faith.
- Every goal I write will reflect Your wisdom, not my pride.
- I will run my race with clarity, endurance, and grace.
- In Jesus' name, Amen.

CHAPTER 9
S.M.A.R.T Goals, Spirit-Led Guidance
Balancing Structure and Surrender

"Trust in the Lord with all your heart; and lean not unto your own understanding. In all your ways acknowledge Him, and He shall direct your paths." — **Proverbs 3:5–6 (KJV)**

Planning is holy when guided by the Holy Spirit. God invites you to use wisdom, order, and diligence—but He also calls you to remain sensitive to His leading. The key to prophetic success lies in this balance: *structure* and *surrender.*

A wise believer plans with clarity but holds every plan loosely enough for God to redirect at any time. This is the heart of Spirit-led goal setting.

Why S.M.A.R.T Goals Still Matter

The world of business and leadership often uses the *S.M.A.R.T* acronym to define strong goals:

S – Specific
M – Measurable
A – Achievable
R – Relevant
T – Time-bound

These principles are useful because they bring structure, clarity, and accountability. But for the prophetic believer, *S.M.A.R.T* must also be *SPIRIT-LED.*

Heavenly wisdom doesn't reject structure—it redeems it.
God is not random; He is orderly.

1 Corinthians 14:40 reminds us, *"Let all things be done decently and in order."*

SPECIFIC — Clarity Unlocks Power

"Write the vision and make it plain…" — **Habakkuk 2:2**

A goal without clarity cannot carry authority.
Be precise about what you're asking God to help you accomplish. Vague goals produce vague results.

Instead of saying, *"I want to grow spiritually,"* write, "I will spend 30 minutes each morning in prayer and Bible reading."

Specificity transforms your intentions into actionable faith. When you know *what* to do, you can trust God with *how* to do it.

Spirit-Led Question:
Holy Spirit, what specific instruction are You giving me in this season?

MEASURABLE — Track God's Faithfulness

Measurable goals are not about performance; they are about progress.

God often brings growth in gradual steps. Measuring helps you see His hand at work over time.

For example:

- Instead of saying, "I'll start giving more," write, "I will set aside 10% of every income for tithes and another 5% for generosity."

- Instead of "I want to write my book," write, "I will complete one chapter every two weeks."

Measurement gives you markers of accountability. It also allows you to celebrate God's faithfulness in every small win.

Spirit-Led Question:
Lord, how can I measure progress in a way that glorifies You, not my ego?

ACHIEVABLE — Faithful, Not Fantastical

Achievable does *not* mean small—it means realistic given your season, capacity, and resources.

God may reveal a massive long-term vision, but He will guide you to pursue it one obedient step at a time. Remember:
Noah didn't build the ark in a week.
Joseph didn't rule Egypt overnight.
David didn't become king immediately after being anointed.

The Holy Spirit leads us *progressively*.
Faith doesn't ignore practical limits—it trusts God to expand them in time.

> **Start where you are, with what you have, in the strength you've been given.**

Spirit-Led Question:
Lord, what step can I take now that is both faithful and feasible?

RELEVANT — Aligned with Heaven's Agenda

Not every good goal is a God goal.
Relevance means your goals must align with your divine assignment and current season.

Ask:
- Does this goal move me closer to my God-given vision?
- Does it strengthen my relationship with God or serve others?
- Or is it a distraction disguised as opportunity?

Even Jesus said in **John 17:4**, *"I have finished the work which You gave Me to do."*

Not every task is yours to complete. Prophetic relevance means focusing on what Heaven has assigned specifically to *you*.

Spirit-Led Question:
Holy Spirit, is this goal part of my current assignment?

TIME-BOUND — Partnering with God's Timing

God operates in appointed times and seasons (**Ecclesiastes 3:1**).

Setting time frames keeps you attentive to His rhythm.

Time-bound goals build urgency and discipline. They also help you discern whether you're waiting on God—or simply procrastinating. However, avoid turning timelines into ultimatums. God's timing is perfect even when it differs from yours.

When your due date meets His divine date, breakthrough happens.

Spirit-Led Question:
Lord, what is Your appointed time for this goal? Help me to move neither ahead nor behind You.

S.M.A.R.T + SPIRIT Framework

Here's how the redeemed model might look:

S.M.A.R.T	SPIRIT-LED BALANCE
Specific	Seek clarity through prayer and revelation.
Measurable	Track progress while trusting divine process.
Achievable	Take faithful steps while believing for expansion.
Relevant	Align every goal with Kingdom purpose.
Time-bound	Respect seasons but remain flexible to God's timing.

When you merge structure with surrender, your planning becomes worship.

S.M.A.R.T. in Practice — A Prophetic Example

Let's say your **vision** is: *"To teach and mentor young adults in prophetic living."*

Your **S.M.A.R.T, Spirit-Led Goal** might look like this:
- **Specific:** Launch a 6-week online teaching series on hearing God's voice.
- **Measurable:** Enroll at least 20 participants and hold one live session per week.
- **Achievable:** Prepare all lessons and outlines within the next 30 days.
- **Relevant:** This aligns directly with my call to equip believers prophetically.
- **Time-bound:** Begin the first session by March 1 and complete by mid-April.

This goal is structured, yet open to divine redirection if the Holy Spirit reveals a better format or timing.

Letting God Override the Plan

No plan, no matter how well written, replaces God's voice.

Isaiah 55:8–9 reminds us: *"My thoughts are not your thoughts, neither are your ways My ways."*

As you plan, stay sensitive to interruptions. Sometimes what feels like a detour is actually divine redirection.

Your flexibility is a form of faith—it says, *"Lord, I trust Your wisdom more than my plan."*

When God changes your direction, He's not confusing you; He's *protecting* you.

Reflection — When Structure Meets Surrender

1. Which area of the S.M.A.R.T model do you find easiest? Which is hardest?

   _____

   _____

   _____

   _____

2. How has the Holy Spirit redirected your plans in the past—and what did you learn?

   _____

   _____

   _____

   _____

3. How can you maintain accountability while still leaving room for divine surprise?

   _____

_____

_____

_____

Take time to journal your answers. Allow the Holy Spirit to reveal where you may need more structure—or more surrender.

Prophetic Declaration

- Father, I thank You for divine order and Spirit-led wisdom.
- I commit to planning with clarity, diligence, and flexibility.
- My goals will be S.M.A.R.T and Spirit-filled—specific yet surrendered, measurable yet merciful.
- I trust You to direct every step and adjust every plan according to Your perfect will.
- I will walk in balance—disciplined yet dependent, focused yet free.
- In Jesus' name, Amen.

CHAPTER 10
Categories and Timing
Understanding Divine Seasons and Goal Alignment

"To everything there is a season, and a time to every purpose under heaven." — **Ecclesiastes 3:1 (KJV)**

You can have a powerful vision and perfectly written goals yet still feel stuck if you miss *timing*.

Every assignment has an appointed moment. Just as crops grow in seasons, destiny unfolds in stages. Wisdom is knowing *what* to pursue—and *when* to pursue it.

The Rhythm of Heaven

God's Kingdom moves in rhythm, not rush.
When you align with that rhythm, your effort becomes effective instead of exhausting.

Timing is the divine filter through which God protects both you and the promise.

Sometimes He delays because your capacity isn't ready; other times, He accelerates because grace has come for a specific task.

When you move in God's time, even hard things flow with ease.

Understanding Seasons of Life

Every believer cycles through distinct spiritual seasons. Recognizing yours prevents frustration and comparison.

1. **The Planting Season** — You receive vision, instruction, and preparation. This is where foundations form.

2. **The Growing Season** — You build consistency, develop skill, and learn obedience. Progress may be slow but steady.

3. **The Pruning Season** — God removes distractions, wrong motives, or relationships that hinder fruit. Painful, but purifying.

4. **The Harvest Season** — Manifestation comes. You see visible results and testimonies from previous obedience.

You can be in harvest in one area (career) and planting in another (relationships). Discern each area individually.

Goal Categories for a Whole Life

Prophetic goal setting isn't limited to ministry or finances—it covers every dimension of the believer's life. God cares about your *whole person*.

Here are seven categories to help you structure your goals prayerfully:

1. **Spiritual Goals**
   Deepen intimacy with God.
   Examples: consistent prayer schedule, Bible study plan, fasting rhythm, serving in ministry.

2. **Personal Growth Goals**
   Strengthen mind and character.
   Examples: reading plan, new skill development, overcoming a personal fear, emotional healing work.

3. **Health & Wellness Goals**
   Steward the temple of the Holy Spirit.
   Examples: nutrition discipline, daily exercise, better rest patterns, mental-health care.

4. **Financial Goals**
   Build stability and generosity.
   Examples: debt repayment, saving target, business expansion, tithing consistency.

5. **Relational Goals**
   Cultivate godly connections and harmony.
   Examples: restoring family unity, mentoring relationships, building community, setting healthy boundaries.

6. **Vocational / Ministry Goals**
   Advance your calling and service.
   Examples: launching a ministry, writing curriculum, workplace evangelism, leadership training.

7. **Kingdom Impact Goals**
   Extend God's love beyond yourself.
   Examples: missions support, charity work, mentoring youth, prophetic intercession networks.

When you categorize your goals, you see the fullness of how God desires to bless and use you.

How to Prioritize by Timing

1. **Ask for Heaven's Calendar**
   Pray, *"Lord, what is for now, what is for later, and what should wait?"*

2. **Discern Urgency vs. Importance**
   Urgent tasks scream for attention; important ones build destiny. Choose importance over noise.

3. **Sequence by Season**
   Some goals require foundation before fruition. You can't harvest before you plant.
   Example: Don't launch a new ministry until you've built prayer consistency.

4. **Set Quarterly Focus**
   Divide the year into four quarters. Assign 1–2 major goals per season rather than scattering energy everywhere.

5. **Stay Flexible**
   If God shifts timing, adjust gracefully. Flexibility is faith in motion.

Signs You're Out of Alignment

- Constant frustration despite obedience.
- Lack of grace or joy in the work.
- Closed doors that used to open easily.
- Anxiety instead of peace when acting.

When these appear, pause and re-evaluate. You may be doing the right thing—but in the wrong time. Go back to prayer, and ask, *"Lord, am I early, late, or exactly where You want me?"*

Practical Exercise: Mapping Your Prophetic Calendar

1. Draw a circle divided into four quarters (Spring – Summer – Fall – Winter).

2. In each section, write one or two goals from different categories.

3. Pray over each quarter, asking the Holy Spirit to confirm or reorder your plans.

4. Keep this map visible in your journal or on a vision board.

This simple exercise helps you pace yourself and avoid burnout.

Reflection — Walking in God's Timing

1. Which season do you sense you're currently in: planting, growing, pruning, or harvest?

   _____

   _____

   _____

   _____

2. Which category of your life most needs balance or renewed focus?

   _____

   _____

   _____

   _____

3. Where might you need to wait—and where might God be calling you to act now?

   _____

   _____

   _____

   _____

Journal your answers, then pray for alignment before adjusting any plans.

Prophetic Declaration

- Father, thank You for divine timing.
- I refuse to run ahead or lag behind.
- Teach me to recognize my seasons and steward them wisely.
- Every area of my life will flow in harmony with Your calendar.
- I will move with grace, build with diligence, and rest with trust.
- In Jesus' name, Amen.

CHAPTER 11
Prophetic Goal-Setting Prompts
Spirit-Led Templates for Practical Action

"The plans of the diligent lead surely to abundance, but everyone who is hasty comes only to poverty." — **Proverbs 21:5 (ESV)**

Prophetic people don't just dream—they design. Once you have discerned your season and categories, it's time to write *Spirit-led goals* that you can act on. These prompts will help you translate revelation into responsible steps while staying sensitive to the Holy Spirit.

Each prompt below uses the **S.M.A.R.T.** pattern (Specific | Measurable | Achievable | Relevant | Time-Bound) infused with prayer and prophecy. Think of them as **templates for dialogue** with God, not mechanical worksheets.

Prompt 1 — Spiritual Growth & Intimacy

Scripture Focus: Joshua 1:8
"This Book of the Law shall not depart from your mouth... for then you will make your way prosperous."

Ask:
- Lord, what new rhythm of prayer, study, or worship are You inviting me into?
- How can I deepen my awareness of Your presence daily?

Template Example:
- **Specific:** I will spend 30 minutes each morning in prayer and Scripture before checking messages.
- **Measurable:** Track consistency for 30 days.
- **Achievable:** Wake 30 minutes earlier; set phone to "Do Not Disturb."
- **Relevant:** Strengthens intimacy with God and clarity for my calling.
- **Time-Bound:** Begin Monday; review results at month's end.

Small moments of devotion open large doors of revelation.

Prompt 2 — Personal Development & Mind Renewal

Scripture Focus: Romans 12:2
"Be transformed by the renewing of your mind."

Ask:
- What limiting belief is God challenging me to replace with truth?
- What new skill or knowledge will help me steward my calling?

Template Example:
- **Specific:** Read one book each month on leadership and prophetic discernment.
- **Measurable:** Keep a summary page per book.
- **Achievable:** 20 minutes reading per day.
- **Relevant:** Prepares me for mentoring others.
- **Time-Bound:** Complete four books this quarter.

Education becomes elevation when guided by revelation.

Prompt 3 — Health and Wholeness

Scripture Focus: 3 John 1:2
"Beloved, I wish above all things that thou mayest prosper and be in health, even as thy soul prospereth."

Ask:
- What one physical habit would honor the temple of the Holy Spirit?
- How is my rest, diet, or exercise affecting my spiritual clarity?

Template Example:
- **Specific:** Walk 30 minutes five days each week while praying in tongues or listening to worship.
- **Measurable:** Track walks in planner.
- **Achievable:** Schedule after work; prepare shoes in advance.
- **Relevant:** Restores energy for ministry.
- **Time-Bound:** Maintain for 8 weeks, then reassess.

Physical alignment supports prophetic endurance.

Prompt 4 — Financial Stewardship and Generosity

Scripture Focus: Deuteronomy 8:18
"It is He who gives you power to get wealth, that He may establish His covenant."

Ask:
- Lord, how can I honor You with my finances this year?
- What debts, disciplines, or giving goals should I prioritize?

Template Example:
- **Specific:** Create a monthly budget that includes tithe, savings, and giving fund.
- **Measurable:** Review spending every two weeks.
- **Achievable:** Use an app or spreadsheet.
- **Relevant:** Builds integrity and freedom for Kingdom generosity.
- **Time-Bound:** Budget finalized by month end; 3-month trial.

Generosity keeps your heart light enough to hear God clearly.

Prompt 5 — Relationships and Community

Scripture Focus: Proverbs 27:17
"As iron sharpens iron, so one person sharpens another."

Ask:
- Who is God calling me to reconcile with or invest in?
- How can I build community that strengthens Kingdom purpose?

Template Example:
- **Specific:** Host a monthly dinner or prayer circle for spiritual friends.

- **Measurable:** Track attendance and shared testimonies.
- **Achievable:** Schedule first gathering within four weeks.
- **Relevant:** Creates accountability and fellowship.
- **Time-Bound:** Continue for six months, then evaluate impact.

When the right people gather, new grace flows.

Prompt 6 — Ministry or Career Assignment

Scripture Focus: Colossians 3:23
"Whatever you do, work heartily, as for the Lord."

Ask:
- What project or assignment most reflects my divine purpose this year?
- How can I serve with excellence where I am planted?

Template Example:
- **Specific:** Develop and launch a 6-week online course on prophetic goal setting.
- **Measurable:** Prepare content schedule; measure engagement and testimonies.
- **Achievable:** Dedicate two evenings weekly to preparation.
- **Relevant:** Directly fulfills my teaching mandate.
- **Time-Bound:** Launch by September 1.

Your diligence becomes someone else's deliverance.

Prompt 7 — Kingdom Impact and Legacy

Scripture Focus: Matthew 5:16
"Let your light so shine before men, that they may see your good works and glorify your Father."

Ask:
- How will my obedience bless generations after me?
- What cause or community can I uplift through service or giving?

Template Example:
- **Specific:** Partner with one local youth program to mentor quarterly.
- **Measurable:** Track mentee progress and feedback.
- **Achievable:** Two hours per session.
- **Relevant:** Invests prophetic wisdom into the next generation.
- **Time-Bound:** Begin January; complete four sessions by year-end.

Legacy is not what you leave *to* people—it's what you leave *in* them.

Turning Prompts into a Living Plan

After completing all seven prompts:

1. **Pray for Confirmation.** Ask the Holy Spirit to highlight which goals are *now* assignments and which are *next*.

2. **Record in One Place.** Use a prophetic planner or journal to track prayer, progress, and testimony.

3. **Review Quarterly.** Realign as seasons shift.

4. **Rejoice in Growth.** Progress, not perfection, is the evidence of grace.

   Every obedient action is a prophetic declaration in motion.

Reflection — From Paper to Purpose

1. Which prompt stirred the strongest sense of urgency or excitement?

   _____

   _____

   _____

2. What resource or relationship might help you complete one key goal?

_____

_____

_____

_____

3. What fear or habit could hinder your follow-through—and how will you confront it?

_____

_____

_____

_____

Write your reflections beneath each prompt to keep them personal and prayerful.

Prophetic Declaration

- Father, thank You for wisdom that turns revelation into action.
- I commit every plan to You—my spiritual, personal, and practical goals.
- Breathe on each step with Your Spirit.
- Let diligence meet grace, and structure meet surrender.
- I will walk out these goals in joy, integrity, and obedience.

- In Jesus' name, Amen.

CHAPTER 12
Prayer Points for Divine Direction
Covering Your Goals in Intercession

"The effectual fervent prayer of a righteous man availeth much." — **James 5:16 (KJV)**

Every prophetic goal requires prophetic prayer. It's not enough to plan well—you must *pray through*. Your plans may begin on paper, but they are sustained through prayer.

Prayer keeps your heart sensitive, your motives pure, and your focus aligned with Heaven.

Without intercession, even the best goals risk drifting into self-effort. With prayer, ordinary plans become *supernatural assignments.*

Why Every Goal Needs Prayer

Prayer is not a backup plan; it's the blueprint of success.

When you pray, you aren't trying to convince God to bless your plan—you're inviting Him to **breathe on it.**

Prayer does three things for your goals:

1. **It clarifies direction** — revealing what truly matters in each season.

2. **It sanctifies motives** — ensuring you pursue purpose, not pride.

3. **It releases divine empowerment** — turning effort into grace-filled achievement.

When you cover your plans in prayer, they stop being *your* plans and become *His*.

> **You don't need more strength—you need more surrender.**

How to Pray Over Your Goals

1. **Present Them with Thanksgiving**
   Thank God for the privilege of having a vision at all. Gratitude turns anxiety into assurance. **(Philippians 4:6–7)**

2. **Invite the Holy Spirit's Direction**
   Ask Him to refine or rewrite anything that isn't aligned with God's will.

3. **Pray the Word**
   Find Scripture that supports each category of your goals. The Word is your legal authority in Heaven's court.

4. **Listen as Much as You Speak**
   Prayer is conversation, not monologue. Make room for revelation.

5. **Declare with Confidence**
   Speak faith-filled decrees over your written plans. Words activate what worship conceives.

6. **End with Worship**
   Close every planning session in praise. Worship re-centers your heart around the One who gave the vision.

Seven Core Prayer Points for Prophetic Goal Setters

Each prayer point includes a Scripture base and a short sample prayer. Use these daily or weekly to keep your goals spiritually fortified.

1. Prayer for Alignment

Scripture: *"In all your ways acknowledge Him, and He will direct your paths."* — **Proverbs 3:6**

Prayer:
- Lord, I surrender my ambitions to You.
- Let every goal align with Your perfect will.
- Redirect anything born of self-will, and confirm every plan rooted in obedience.
- Make my steps straight and my motives pure.

2. Prayer for Wisdom and Strategy

Scripture: *"If any of you lacks wisdom, let him ask of God."* — **James 1:5**

Prayer:
- Father, release divine strategy for every assignment.
- Show me the how, not just the what.

- Grant me discernment for timing, structure, and partnerships.
- Let Heaven's blueprints guide every earthly decision.

3. Prayer for Strength and Endurance

Scripture: *"Be strong in the Lord and in the power of His might."* — **Ephesians 6:10**

Prayer:
- Lord, strengthen my hands for the work You've given me.
- When I grow weary, renew my spirit.
- Help me to persevere with joy, not strive with anxiety.
- I receive Your supernatural stamina for every season.

4. Prayer for Provision

Scripture: *"My God shall supply all your need according to His riches in glory."* — **Philippians 4:19**

Prayer:
- Jehovah Jireh, thank You for being my Source.
- Open doors of divine provision—resources, favor, and opportunity.
- Let lack never limit my obedience.
- I trust You to finance what You've called me to build.

5. Prayer for Protection

Scripture: *"No weapon formed against you shall prosper."* — **Isaiah 54:17**

Prayer:
- Father, I declare divine protection over my mind, my work, and my relationships.
- Shield my goals from sabotage, distraction, or discouragement.
- Guard me from fear and preserve my peace.
- Surround me with angelic covering as I advance.

6. Prayer for Fruitfulness

Scripture: *"He shall be like a tree planted by the rivers of water, that brings forth fruit in its season."* — **Psalm 1:3**

Prayer:
- Lord, let everything I plant in obedience bear fruit.
- Cause my labor to prosper and my impact to multiply.
- May souls be touched, lives changed, and Your glory revealed.
- Keep me rooted in Your Word as I grow.

7. Prayer for Divine Timing

Scripture: *"For the vision is yet for an appointed time."* — **Habakkuk 2:3**

Prayer:
- God of perfect timing, help me move with Your rhythm.
- Silence impatience and fear of delay.
- When You say wait, I will rest; when You say move, I will run.
- Align my pace with Your prophetic calendar.

The Role of Fasting in Prophetic Goal Setting

Fasting sharpens spiritual sensitivity. It quiets the noise of the flesh so you can hear God's strategy clearly. Consider setting aside a day or a meal each week to pray over your goals specifically. Use that time to intercede, review progress, and invite course corrections.

> **Fasting doesn't earn favor—it enhances focus.**

How to Build a "Prayer Shield" Around Your Plans

1. **Create a Prayer Circle.**
   Share key goals with two or three trusted intercessors who can cover you.

2. **Schedule Weekly Prayer Time.**
   Treat it as seriously as meetings or deadlines.

3. **Record Answers.**
   Keep a "Prayer Journal for Results." Seeing answered prayers builds faith for the next step.

4. **Celebrate Breakthroughs.**
   Gratitude attracts more grace. Each testimony fuels new courage.

Reflection — Listening Before Launching

1. What goal do you sense needs more prayer before execution?

   _____

   _____

   _____

   _____

2. How can you build a consistent rhythm of intercession for your plans?

   _____

   _____

   _____

   _____

3. Who can join you in prayer agreement this season?

   _____

   _____

   _____

Prophetic Declaration

- Father, I dedicate every plan to You in prayer.
- Let my intercession be as incense before Your throne.
- Breathe life into my goals, wisdom into my mind, and peace into my pace.
- I will not move without Your guidance, nor fear when You command me to go.
- My goals are covered by grace and guided by glory.
- In Jesus' name, Amen.

CHAPTER 13
Living in the Overflow
Maintaining Consistency, Gratitude, and Grace in Success

"You anoint my head with oil; my cup runs over." — **Psalm 23:5 (KJV)**

Overflow is not just having more; it's *becoming more.* It's the state of living in continual awareness of God's presence and provision—where every part of your life reflects His abundance.

Prophetic goal setting is not only about achieving outcomes but cultivating a lifestyle of alignment, stewardship, and thanksgiving. The true reward of success in the Kingdom is not status—it's *sustainability*.

What It Means to "Live in the Overflow"

Overflow is when what God does *in you* exceeds what's needed *for you*, and begins to pour out *through you*.

It's the shift from survival to stewardship—from praying for blessing to becoming a blessing.

Jesus said, *"I have come that they may have life, and have it more abundantly."* **(John 10:10)**

That abundant life (*zoē* in Greek—the God-kind of life) includes peace, purpose, provision, and presence.

Overflow is not about excess; it's about *expression*—the outward demonstration of inward transformation.

> **True success is overflow under control.**

The Spiritual Danger of Arrival

Every vision fulfilled carries a hidden test: *Can you remain humble when it happens?*

It's easy to depend on God when you're waiting; harder when things start working. Many believers unknowingly drift from grace once they taste success.

Deuteronomy 8:18 warns us:

"Remember the Lord your God, for it is He who gives you power to get wealth."

Never forget the Source behind your success. Keep gratitude louder than achievement. Your ability to remain thankful determines how long the blessing remains fruitful.

Signs You're Losing Alignment

- You start protecting reputation more than revelation.
- Prayer becomes optional rather than essential.
- Goals replace intimacy.
- Fruit increases but joy decreases.

The antidote is simple:

Return to the posture of worship that birthed your vision in the first place.

Consistency: The Secret to Continual Growth

Consistency is the bridge between seasons. It's how you move from grace to greater grace without burnout.

Most people fail not from lack of passion, but from lack of *patterns*.

Consistency Keys

1. **Routine with Revelation** — Create daily habits (prayer, planning, rest) that support your calling.

2. **Review Regularly** — Assess monthly: *What's working? What's drifting? What needs pruning?*

3. **Stay Accountable** — Share progress with a mentor or prayer partner.

4. **Protect Your Sabbath** — Rest is a weapon. Renewal is not laziness—it's leadership.

Consistency is the quiet miracle that turns obedience into overflow.

Gratitude: The Guardian of Abundance

Gratitude multiplies what grace provides.
Jesus demonstrated this principle when He gave thanks for five loaves and two fish—and they fed thousands. (John 6:11)

Whatever you thank God for increases in value and longevity.

Gratitude keeps your spirit soft, your motives pure, and your focus upward.

Daily Gratitude Practice

- Begin every morning with three thank-yous before three requests.
- Journal weekly about answered prayers and hidden blessings.
- Verbally thank those who have helped you along the way.
- Celebrate small wins; they are evidence of large faithfulness.

When gratitude becomes habit, overflow becomes lifestyle.

Grace for the Next Season

Grace doesn't just forgive—it *empowers*.
You began this journey by grace, and you will finish by grace.

2 Corinthians 9:8 says,

"And God is able to make all grace abound toward you; that you, always having all sufficiency in all things, may abound to every good work."

That means there's grace for every phase: the waiting, the working, and the winning.
When you live in overflow, you don't stop depending on grace—you depend more deeply. You recognize that every success is sustained by the same mercy that started your vision.

Overflow is not independence—it's deeper dependence.

Giving Back: The Fruit of Fulfillment

When God brings you into your "promised land," He expects you to sow back into others.

Your success was never meant to terminate with you—it's a trust to distribute.

Ask yourself:
- Who can I mentor with what I've learned?
- How can my increase fund Kingdom purpose?
- Where can my story bring someone else hope?

Luke 6:38 promises, *"Give, and it shall be given unto you."*

Generosity keeps your flow open. The more you pour out, the more God pours in.

Maintaining the Overflow Mindset

- **Stay Teachable:** Keep learning. Arrogance clogs abundance.

- **Stay Available:** Be open for new assignments. Every season holds fresh purpose.

- **Stay Holy:** Purity protects prosperity.

- **Stay Joyful:** Joy keeps the flow alive, complaining stops it.

- **Stay Expectant:** Believe that the best is still ahead.

Your vision may have come to pass, but God is not finished writing your story.

Reflection — Sustaining the Season of Blessing

1. What habits helped you reach this point—and which ones will help you sustain it?

_____

_____

_____

_____

2. Who could benefit from your experience or mentorship?

_____

_____

_____

_____

3. How can you intentionally express gratitude this week?

_____

_____

_____

_____

Take a moment to thank God for every fulfilled goal, every delayed prayer that matured you, and every open door that revealed His faithfulness.

Prophetic Declaration

- Father, I thank You for the overflow of Your grace in my life.
- I will not grow proud in blessing, nor weary in well-doing.
- I live from abundance, not anxiety—from gratitude, not greed.
- My cup runs over, and I pour into others with joy.

- I will remain consistent, grateful, and full of grace for every season ahead.
- In Jesus' name, Amen.

PART III:
Walking in Divine Alignment — The Life of a Visionary Believer

CHAPTER 14
Walking in Alignment
Living as a Visionary Every Day

"Can two walk together, except they be agreed?" — **Amos 3:3 (KJV)**

Walking in divine alignment is about agreement — not just believing in God, but *moving with Him.*

It's living in sync with Heaven's rhythm, where every step is a response to His leading.

You were never meant to live reactively, chasing circumstances or trends. You were designed to live prophetically — walking in daily awareness that your life is unfolding according to divine design.

When you walk in alignment, peace becomes your compass, purpose your path, and obedience your pace.

Alignment Is Agreement

Alignment begins with *agreement.*

To be in alignment with God means to say yes not only to His promises, but also to His process.
Sometimes we agree with the prophecy but resist the preparation.
We celebrate the destination but question the direction.

But true alignment says, *"Lord, I'll walk where You lead — even when I don't understand why."*

Every time you choose obedience over comfort, you're walking in alignment.

Every time you surrender pride for purpose, you're saying yes to divine partnership.

Your steps reveal your agreement more than your words do.

The Three Dimensions of Alignment

To walk as a visionary believer, you must align in three areas: **spirit, soul, and body.**

Spiritual Alignment

- Stay connected to God through prayer, worship, and the Word.

- Make intimacy your anchor, not activity.

- Let the Holy Spirit remain your primary voice in every decision.

Soul Alignment

- Renew your mind daily. (**Romans 12:2**)

- Guard your emotions from bitterness, comparison, and fear.

- Keep your will submitted to God's will — even when it conflicts with your plans.

Physical Alignment

- Manage your health, schedule, and environment.

- Create boundaries that protect your peace and productivity.

- Remember: a tired body can't carry a fresh anointing.

When all three dimensions align, clarity flows and confusion loses its grip.

Alignment Produces Acceleration

When your heart and habits agree with Heaven, momentum follows.

Alignment removes resistance — both spiritual and practical. That's why God often slows us down before speeding us up. He adjusts our priorities, relationships, and routines so that when the blessing comes, we're ready to carry it.

Think of alignment like tuning an instrument. When you're in tune, even small movements produce beautiful sound. But when you're off-key, even loud effort sounds strained.

The goal isn't noise — it's harmony.

> **Before God amplifies your influence, He fine-tunes your alignment.**

Daily Practices of an Aligned Life

Alignment isn't a one-time decision; it's a daily discipline.

Here are practices that keep your steps steady in every season:

a. Morning Surrender

Begin each day by saying aloud, *"Lord, lead me today. Let my thoughts, words, and actions please You."*

It re-centers your priorities before distractions arrive.

b. Midday Check-In

Pause midway through your day to ask, *"Am I still moving with peace?"*

Peace is the Holy Spirit's navigation system. If it's gone, adjust course.

c. Evening Reflection

End your day by reviewing:

- Where did I see God's hand today?
- Where did I resist His prompting?

Write brief notes in your journal. These reflections build awareness and maturity.

d. Weekly Reset

Set aside a Sabbath or rest period for prayer, planning, and reflection.

Review your goals, celebrate progress, and release frustration. Alignment thrives in rhythm, not rigidity.

Guardrails of Alignment

To remain steady in your walk, you need spiritual *guardrails*—boundaries that protect your focus and integrity.

- **Guard Your Inputs:** What you read, watch, and hear shapes your perception. Feed on the Word more than the world.

- **Guard Your Relationships:** Stay close to people who value your purpose. Distance from dishonor preserves your destiny.

- **Guard Your Thoughts:** Every great detour starts as a thought. Capture negative or fearful ideas before they take root.

- **Guard Your Rest:** Busyness is often the enemy of alignment. Stillness restores sight.

The Power of Continual Yes

The visionary believer doesn't just say "yes" once — they live in a continual yes.

Every new level of purpose will require a fresh surrender.

Jesus modeled this perfectly. In Gethsemane, He prayed, *"Not My will, but Yours be done."* That one act of surrender changed eternity.

Each time you say yes to God's will over your own, you move closer to your divine design.

Your "yes" today sustains the vision tomorrow.

Obedience is how you keep the door of destiny open.

Walking With God in Every Environment

Alignment doesn't end when you leave church; it continues at work, home, and everywhere in between. The same Spirit who speaks in your prayer closet guides you in the boardroom, the classroom, and the living room.

Learn to invite God into every space:

- *"Holy Spirit, help me respond with grace in this conversation."*
- *"Father, show me how to solve this problem creatively."*
- *"Jesus, teach me to serve humbly even when unseen."*

This is the prophetic life — not mystical distance from reality, but spiritual awareness within it.

The prophetic life is not about escaping the world, but transforming it through alignment.

Reflection — Walking in Daily Agreement

1. In what area of life (spirit, soul, or body) do you sense the greatest misalignment right now?

   _____
   _____
   _____
   _____

2. What daily rhythm or practice could help restore that balance?

   _____
   _____
   _____
   _____

3. How will you remain sensitive to God's direction amid busy routines?

   _____
   _____
   _____

Pause and journal your responses. Then pray for fresh alignment before you move forward.

Prophetic Declaration

- Father, I choose to walk in divine alignment every day.
- Let my spirit, soul, and body move in harmony with Your purpose.
- I say yes again to Your will, even when I don't see the full picture.
- Order my steps, refine my heart, and tune my pace to Heaven's rhythm.
- May my walk be steady, my heart pure, and my life a reflection of Your grace.
- In Jesus' name, Amen.

CHAPTER 15
The Rewards of Alignment
Peace, Purpose, and Prophetic Power

"You will keep in perfect peace all who trust in You, all whose thoughts are fixed on You." — **Isaiah 26:3 (NLT)**

When you walk in step with Heaven, reward is not something you chase—it's something that follows.

Divine alignment brings fruit that no striving can manufacture: inner peace, clear purpose, and prophetic power.

These are not prizes for perfection; they are by-products of proximity to God.

Peace — The Signature of God's Presence

Peace is Heaven's confirmation that you're walking in the right direction. It doesn't mean every circumstance is calm—it means your *spirit* is.

Philippians 4:7 calls it *"the peace of God, which surpasses all understanding."*

When your mind wants to panic but your heart stays still, that's the mark of alignment.

Living in Peace Looks Like:

- Making decisions without fear or pressure.

- Letting go of outcomes once you've obeyed.

- Refusing to compete or compare.

- Resting even while responsibilities remain.

Peace is not the absence of problems—it's the awareness of Presence.

If your peace disappears, don't press harder; pause. It's the Holy Spirit's gentle nudge to realign.

Purpose — The Fulfillment of Obedience

Purpose is discovered, not invented.

It unfolds as you obey one instruction at a time. Alignment keeps you close enough to hear those instructions clearly.

When you live on purpose:

- Ordinary tasks gain eternal meaning.

- Your "why" becomes stronger than your "when."
- Confusion gives way to conviction.

Ephesians 2:10 reminds us, *"We are His workmanship, created in Christ Jesus for good works."*

Those works are already prepared—you simply walk into them as you stay aligned.

> **Purpose is not a destination; it's the joy of daily obedience.**

Prophetic Power — The Overflow of Relationship

Alignment doesn't just keep you peaceful; it makes you powerful.

When you remain close to God, His authority flows through you naturally.

Jesus said, *"I only do what I see My Father doing."* **(John 5:19)**

That statement reveals the secret of prophetic power—*intimacy-based action.*

Signs of Prophetic Power

- You speak with wisdom that surprises even you.
- Doors open without manipulation.
- Your prayers shift atmospheres.
- Miracles happen in ordinary places.

Power without intimacy becomes performance; power with alignment becomes transformation.

> **Prophetic power is the natural result of prophetic proximity.**

The Compound Effect of Alignment

Each reward multiplies the others:

Peace stabilizes you.
Purpose focuses you.
Power propels you.

Together, they create a life of momentum and meaning—a testimony that God's way truly works. People notice when you live this way; your calm becomes contagious, your clarity magnetic, your authority undeniable.

That influence isn't about fame—it's about *fruit*.

When Alignment Feels Costly

Sometimes staying aligned costs relationships, opportunities, or comfort. But anything you lose for the sake of obedience becomes seed for greater harvest.

Mark 10:29-30 promises that whoever sacrifices for Christ will receive *"a hundredfold now in this time... and in the world to come eternal life."*

Your temporary losses protect eternal gain.

> **Obedience may be expensive, but misalignment is unaffordable.**

Sustaining the Rewards

- **Stay Rooted in the Word.** Scripture anchors your peace when emotions fluctuate.

- **Stay Accountable.** Alignment thrives in community; isolation breeds deception.

- **Stay Grateful.** Gratitude keeps your heart soft so peace can dwell.

- **Stay Teachable.** The moment you stop learning, you start drifting.

Reflection — Recognizing the Fruit

1. Where do you currently feel the strongest sense of peace?

   _____
   _____
   _____
   _____

2. How has obedience recently clarified your sense of purpose?

   _____
   _____
   _____

3. What evidence of God's power have surfaced as you've stayed aligned?

_____

_____

_____

_____

Journal these signs of growth—they're milestones of maturity.

Prophetic Declaration

- Father, thank You for the rewards that flow from walking with You.
- I receive Your peace that stills every storm, Your purpose that gives my life direction, and Your power that confirms Your Word through me.
- Keep me humble in success, steadfast in obedience, and sensitive to Your Spirit.
- Let my life be living proof that alignment with You produces abundance in every way.
- In Jesus' name, Amen.

CHAPTER 16
Finishing Strong
Enduring Faith and the Legacy of Vision

"I have fought the good fight, I have finished the race, I have kept the faith." — **2 Timothy 4:7 (NKJV)**

Every God-given vision begins with revelation, grows through obedience, and matures through endurance.

Finishing strong means you refuse to stop at inspiration—you persevere until manifestation.

It's not how loud you start that matters; it's how faithfully you finish.

Heaven doesn't applaud speed—it rewards *stewardship*.

The Faith to Finish

Faith doesn't just start things—it sustains them.
When opposition rises, faith whispers, *"Keep going. The promise still stands."*

Hebrews 10:36 reminds us,

"You have need of endurance, so that after you have done the will of God, you may receive the promise."
Every vision will face storms. Your faith is not proven in the launching, but in the lasting.
When everything seems still or slow, remember you are not stuck—you're *being strengthened*.

Enduring faith doesn't avoid resistance—it grows through it.

Lessons from Finishers in Scripture

Noah — Finished the ark despite ridicule. His obedience saved a generation.

Moses — Though flawed, he led Israel to the edge of promise through perseverance.

Paul — Faced imprisonment and persecution, yet completed his assignment with joy.

Jesus — The ultimate finisher, who declared on the cross, *"It is finished."*

Each finisher demonstrates this truth: when you remain faithful to the end, your obedience outlives you.

The Power of Endurance

Endurance is more than patience—it's *pressured faith*. It's believing when nothing is changing, trusting when you can't trace God's hand.

Romans 5:3–4 says,

"Tribulation produces perseverance; and perseverance, character; and character, hope."

Every delay develops something deeper within you. Before God fulfills His promise through you, He perfects His character *in* you.

Waiting time is not wasted time—it's workshop time.

Finishing Requires Focus

Distraction is the enemy of destiny.

As your vision gains momentum, new opportunities may appear that look good—but not all good things are God things.

Stay focused on the *assignment* you've been given. Paul said, *"This one thing I do…"* (**Philippians 3:13**). Finishing requires narrowing your attention so you don't lose direction.

Ask the Holy Spirit daily:

- *What is my assignment for this season?*
- *What no longer aligns with my purpose?*

When you know your "yes," it becomes easier to say "no" to what dilutes it.

The Grace to End Well

Grace that begins a work will also complete it. (**Philippians 1:6**)

You are not finishing in your own strength—you are finishing by divine empowerment.

When weariness comes, rest in this truth:
God never gives a vision without also releasing the grace to fulfill it.

You are not disqualified by fatigue, delay, or even failure. Grace restores momentum.

> **Finishing strong isn't about perfection—it's about persistence in grace.**

The Legacy of Vision

Every fulfilled vision plants seeds for others.
What you build in obedience becomes the foundation for someone else's faith.

Think of Abraham — his faith became a nation.
Think of David — his worship became generations of songs.
Think of Jesus — His sacrifice became salvation for all.

Your obedience has ripple effects far beyond your lifetime.

The books you write, the prayers you pray, the people you mentor—these are all *living legacies*.

> **Legacy is not leaving something behind; it's sending something forward.**

How to Build a Legacy Lifestyle

1. **Mentor the Next Generation.**
   Share your lessons, not just your victories. Transparency teaches better than perfection.

2. **Document the Journey.**
   Keep journals, sermons, and notes. Your testimony will feed those who come after you.

3. **Pass the Vision, Not the Pressure.**
   Inspire others to seek God for their unique assignment—not to replicate yours.

4. **Stay Faithful to the End.**
   There is no retirement from purpose; only transitions from one season to another.

5. **End with Worship.**
   Every finisher sings. Gratitude is the final language of the faithful.

Heaven's Commendation

At the end of every visionary journey awaits one simple phrase worth every sacrifice:

"Well done, good and faithful servant." — **Matthew 25:23**

That is the true measure of success — not numbers, platforms, or applause, but faithfulness.

If you can hear that one sentence from the Father, you've won the only race that matters.

Finishing strong is simply finishing faithful.

Reflection —Your Finisher's Faith

1. What areas of your vision currently require renewed endurance?

   _____
   _____
   _____
   _____

2. Who could benefit from your story or mentorship in this season?

   _____
   _____
   _____
   _____

3. How will you intentionally build legacy as part of your ongoing calling?

   _____
   _____
   _____

Pray over these questions, asking God to mark you as a finisher—faithful to the end.

Prophetic Declaration

- Father, thank You for calling me not just to begin, but to finish strong.
- I receive grace to endure, wisdom to stay focused, and humility to give You all glory.
- Let my obedience echo beyond my lifetime.
- May my life be a legacy of faith, hope, and love.
- When my race is complete, may Heaven rejoice and say, "Well done."
- I finish strong, in Jesus' name, Amen.

Conclusion
The Journey Continues

"Being confident of this very thing, that He who has begun a good work in you will complete it until the day of Jesus Christ." — **Philippians 1:6 (NKJV)**

You've reached the end of this book — but not the end of your story. Prophetic goal setting is not a one-time project; it's a lifelong partnership with God. Each chapter was designed to guide you through revelation, preparation, planning, and alignment — but now, you get to live it.

Every page has been about this simple truth:

God has a plan for your life, and He desires to walk with you as you fulfill it.

You have learned how to receive vision, set faith-filled goals, pray with clarity, act with discipline, and remain aligned in every season. You've written declarations, built prophetic plans, and discovered how to sustain overflow with grace and gratitude.

Now, take a deep breath — and begin walking it out.

The same Spirit who inspired your vision will empower your execution.
The same God who gave you the dream will guide you through the details.

Remember, prophetic living isn't about perfection — it's about *partnership*.

Each day, say again,

> **"Lord, align my plans with Your purpose."**

Let your vision be a continual conversation with Heaven.

> **You are not just a goal-setter; You are a Kingdom builder.**
> **You are not just pursuing success; You are fulfilling prophecy.**

Keep dreaming with God. Keep writing what He says.
Keep living from revelation, not reaction.
The future is not something to fear — it's something to co-create with the One who holds it.

Reflection Journal
Walking Out the Vision

Use this space (or your own journal) to continue your prophetic journey.

Each section includes prompts to help you review, refine, and record what God is doing.

1. Vision Recap

- What is the core vision God has spoken over your life?

  _____

  _____

  _____

  _____

- How has that vision evolved since you began this journey?

  _____

  _____

  _____

  _____

- What signs of progress have you already seen?

2. Goal Alignment Check

- Which goals have you achieved, and how did God show up in the process?

- Which goals need to be refined or delayed for another season?

- Are your goals still aligned with your current assignment?

3. Lessons Learned

- What did this season teach you about faith, patience, or stewardship?

- How did God stretch your character as you pursued your calling?

- What Scriptures or prophetic words became anchors for you?

4. Next Steps

- What is the next phase of your journey?

- What practical steps or spiritual disciplines will you implement?

- Who might God be calling you to mentor or partner with next?

5. Gratitude & Praise

- Write a prayer of thanksgiving for the doors God opened, the strength He gave, and the clarity He provided.

- Record a testimony — even a small one — of His faithfulness during this process.

Testimonies preserve the memory of miracles.

APPENDICES

APPENDIX A
Vision & Goal Setting Worksheets

This appendix provides structured templates, prompts, and exercises to help you apply everything taught in *Prophetic Goal Setting: Aligning Your Vision with God's Plan*.

Use these worksheets during prayer, journaling, planning sessions, or retreats. Return to them throughout the year as God expands, clarifies, or redirects your vision.

A1. VISION CLARITY WORKSHEET

1. What has God shown you about your future?
Write down any dreams, Scriptures, impressions, confirmations, or prophetic words.

_____

_____

_____

_____

2. What desires keep resurfacing in your heart?
God often speaks through repeated burdens or passions.

_____

_____

_____

3. What themes have emerged in prayer this year?
List any recurring spiritual impressions.

_____

_____

_____

_____

4. What problems are you anointed to solve?
Vision often sits where purpose meets burden.

_____

_____

_____

_____

5. What is God calling you to build, birth, or begin?
Business, ministry, book, service, program, relationship, healing journey…

_____

_____

_____

_____

6. What do you sense Heaven is highlighting in this season?

_____

_____

_____

_____

A2. Vision Statement Template

My God-given vision is to…
(Write your vision in one clear, prophetic, faith-filled paragraph.)

_____

_____

_____

_____

Scriptures connected to this vision:
(List the verses God has used to confirm direction.)

_____

_____

_____

Prophetic confirmations received:
(Dreams, words, impressions.)

_____

_____

_____

_____

A3. "Write the Vision" Page

Use this page to rewrite your vision clearly and boldly:
"Write the vision, and make it plain…" — **Habakkuk 2:2**

VISION (Plain Version):

_____

_____

_____

_____

_____

_____

_____

_____

_____
_____
_____
_____
_____

A4. Personal Alignment Audit

Rate yourself from **1–10** in each category:

Category	Score (1–10)	Notes
Spiritual discipline		
Time management		
Emotional health		
Financial stewardship		
Relationships		
Habits & routines		
Faith & obedience		
Focus & consistency		

Reflection Questions:

- Where am I aligned with God's vision?

_____
_____

- Where am I drifting?

- What needs to be strengthened, removed, or prioritized?

A5. Prophetic Goal Planning Pages

These pages help turn vision into action.

1. What is God leading me to accomplish in this season? (Write 3–7 Spirit-led goals.)

_____

_____

_____

2. What steps must I take?

Goal #1:

_____

—

• Step 1

_____

• Step 2

_____

• Step 3

_____

Goal #2:

_____

—

• Step 1

_____

• Step 2

_____

- Step 3 _____

(Repeat as needed.)

A6. Monthly Reflection & Reset Page

Month: _____

1. What did God speak to me this month?

_____

_____

_____

_____

2. What goals progressed?

_____

_____

_____

_____

3. What needs refinement or realignment?

_____

_____

_____

_____

4. What wins can I celebrate?

_____

_____

_____

_____

5. What lessons did I learn?

_____

_____

_____

_____

6. What is God highlighting for next month?

_____

_____

_____

_____

A7. Vision Board Prompt Page

Create a digital or physical vision board using:

- Scriptures

  _____

  _____

- Affirmations

  _____

  _____

  _____

- Images

  _____

  _____

  _____

- Prophetic words

  _____

  _____

  _____

- Personal declarations

    _____

    _____

    _____

    _____

"What do you see?" — Jeremiah 1:11
Place your vision board where you can pray over it regularly.

A8. Annual Prophetic Goal Setting Retreat Guide

Take 1 day, 1 weekend, or a 3-day retreat to:
1. Fast and pray
2. Review the year
3. Seek fresh direction
4. Rewrite your vision
5. Reset your goals
6. Listen for new prophetic instruction

Suggested flow:
1. Worship & Silence
2. Scripture Meditation
3. Vision Review
4. New Vision Download
5. Goal Strategy Session
6. Prayer & Prophetic Declarations

A9. Yearly Prophetic Review Questions

1. What did God fulfill this year?

_____

_____

_____

_____

2. What did I grow through?

3. What shifted in my identity, habits, or routines?

4. What new assignments opened up?

5. What is God closing or ending?

6. What do I need to surrender?

7. What is God preparing me for next?

APPENDIX B
Prayer Templates for Vision & Alignment

These prayers are designed to help readers align their hearts with God's direction and posture themselves spiritually before planning.

B1. PRAYER FOR RECEIVING VISION
"Lord, open the eyes of my spirit. Help me to see what You see concerning my future. Remove confusion, fear, and distraction. Show me Your heart, Your desire, and Your intention for my life. I receive divine clarity in Jesus' name."

B2. PRAYER FOR DISCERNMENT
"Father, give me the ability to distinguish between my desires and Your will. Let the Holy Spirit illuminate what is from You. Silence every voice that does not align with Heaven. Guide me into all truth."

B3. PRAYER FOR DIVINE STRATEGY
"Holy Spirit, teach me how to plan. Give me steps, strategies, and timelines. Help me to move with wisdom, patience, and precision. I welcome Your instruction as I build according to Your pattern."

B4. PRAYER FOR ALIGNMENT
"Lord, bring my mind, emotions, priorities, and habits into alignment with Your vision for my life. Realign whatever has drifted. Strengthen whatever has weakened. Redirect whatever has lost focus."

APPENDIX C
Prophetic Declarations for Vision, Identity & Purpose

C1. Vision Declarations
- I see clearly what God has spoken over my life.
- I am aligned with Heaven's blueprint.
- No confusion can cloud what God has revealed to me.

C2. Identity Declarations
- I am who God says I am.
- I am chosen, equipped, and anointed for purpose.
- I walk in boldness and confidence.

C3. Purpose Declarations
- My steps are ordered by the Lord.
- I walk in divine purpose every day.
- Every assignment connected to my destiny is coming into manifestation.

C4. Prophetic Momentum Declarations
- Vision flows to me.
- Revelation increases in me.
- God's plan is unfolding in my life right now.

APPENDIX D
Prophetic Goal Setting Checklists

D1. Vision Preparation Checklist
Before seeking direction:
- ☐ I have prayed for clarity.
- ☐ I have invited the Holy Spirit to lead.
- ☐ I have quieted my mind and heart.
- ☐ I am willing to surrender personal preferences.
- ☐ I am ready to write what God reveals.

D2. Spiritual Alignment Checklist
- ☐ My heart is clear and forgiven.
- ☐ I am walking in obedience.
- ☐ I am prioritizing spiritual disciplines.
- ☐ I am open to correction and redirection.

D3. Goal Execution Checklist
- ☐ My goals align with Scripture.
- ☐ My goals reflect God's vision for my life.
- ☐ I have realistic timeframes.
- ☐ I have prayerfully chosen my steps.
- ☐ I have removed distractions and unnecessary obligations.

APPENDIX E
Prophetic Prompt Journal Pages

These prompts guide readers into deeper reflection and revelation.

E1. Vision Prompts

"Lord, what are You showing me about my future?"

_____

_____

_____

_____

"What part of my life needs Your clarity?"

_____

_____

_____

_____

"What have You been speaking that I have ignored?"

_____

_____

E2. Alignment Prompts

"Where have I drifted out of alignment?"

"What habits strengthen my purpose?"

"What must I surrender in this season?"

E3. Identity Prompts

"How do You see me, Lord?"

_____

_____

_____

"What lies or fears must I release?"

_____

_____

_____

"What strengths have You placed within me?"

_____

_____

_____

E4. Purpose Prompts

"What problem have You called me to solve?"

_____

_____

_____

_____

"Who am I called to serve?"

_____

_____

_____

_____

"What assignment are You awakening in me now?"

_____

_____

_____

_____

_____

_____

APPENDIX F
Yearly & Quarterly Planning Pages

F1. YEARLY PLANNING OVERVIEW

• Year's Vision Statement

_____

_____

_____

_____

• Top 3 God-led priorities

_____

_____

_____

• Major faith steps

_____

_____

- **Prophetic words received**

  _____

  _____

  _____

  _____

- **Key Scriptures**

  _____

  _____

F2. QUARTERLY OBJECTIVES (Q1–Q4)

- **Quarter Theme**

  Q1 _____

  Q2 _____

  Q3 _____

  Q4 _____

- **Quarter Goals**

  Q1 _____

  Q2 _____

Q3
___

Q4
___

• Major Assignments

Q1
___

Q2
___

Q3
___

Q4
___

• Prayer Focus

Q1
___

Q2
___

Q3
___

Q4
___

• Reflection Notes

Q1
___

Q2
___

Q3
___

Q4

APPENDIX G
Spiritual Warfare & Breakthrough Tools

G1. BREAKING VISION-BLOCKERS
Prayer points for dealing with:

• **Confusion**

_____

_____

• **Distraction**

_____

_____

• **Doubt**

_____

_____

• **Delay**

_____

_____

• **Warfare**

G2. Vision Protection Declarations
- No weapon formed against my purpose will prosper.
- I guard my vision with prayer, discipline, and divine wisdom.
- Every demonic agenda against my clarity is destroyed in Jesus' name.
- I cancel every spirit of distraction assigned to delay or detour my destiny.
- My spiritual sight is protected by the blood of Jesus and cannot be corrupted.
- Every voice that opposes God's plan for my life is silenced now.
- I reject confusion, double-mindedness, and spiritual blindness.
- My God-given vision will not die, fade, or diminish — it will grow stronger.
- Every plot to sabotage my progress is exposed and overturned by God.
- I declare divine protection, clarity, and stability over every step connected to my vision.

Endnotes

Chapter 1 — The Power of Vision
1. Habakkuk 2:2–3 (KJV).
2. Proverbs 29:18 (KJV).
3. Ephesians 1:17–18 (KJV) — Paul's prayer for spiritual eyes to be enlightened.

Chapter 2 — What Is a God-Given Vision?
1. Jeremiah 1:11–12 (KJV) — "What do you see?"
2. Acts 2:17 (KJV) — God pouring out visions and dreams.
3. John 16:13 (KJV) — The Spirit of truth guides into all truth.

Chapter 3 — Vision vs. Goals (or Dreams)
1. Proverbs 16:9 (KJV) — "A man's heart deviseth his way…"
2. Psalm 37:4–5 (KJV) — God shapes the desires of the heart.
3. James 2:17 — Faith without works is dead.

Chapter 4 — The Biblical Blueprint: Writing the Vision
1. Habakkuk 2:2 (KJV) — "Write the vision…"
2. Isaiah 30:8 (KJV) — Writing revelation for future reference.
3. 1 Samuel 3:11 (KJV) — God revealing His intent beforehand.

Chapter 5 — Preparing for Vision: Alignment & Stewardship
1. Psalm 90:12 (KJV) — "Teach us to number our days…"

2. Romans 12:1–2 (KJV) — Transformation begins with renewed thinking.
3. Colossians 3:23–24 (KJV) — Working unto the Lord.

Chapter 6 — Hearing God: Prophetic Goal Setting Prompts
1. John 10:27 (KJV) — "My sheep hear My voice…"
2. Proverbs 3:5–6 (KJV) — God directing paths.
3. Amos 3:7 (KJV) — God reveals His secrets to His servants.

Chapter 7 — Vision Declarations
1. Job 22:28 (KJV) — Decreeing a thing.
2. Mark 11:23 (KJV) — Speaking to mountains.
3. Romans 4:17 (KJV) — Calling those things which be not as though they were.

Chapter 8 — Godly Goals: Moving From Sight to Strategy
1. Joshua 1:8 (KJV) — Prosperity through obedience and meditation.
2. Luke 14:28 (KJV) — Counting the cost.
3. Proverbs 21:5 (KJV) — Plans of the diligent lead to plenty.

Chapter 9 — Spirit-Led Structure & SMART Goals
1. 1 Corinthians 14:40 (KJV) — Doing things decently and in order.
2. Proverbs 16:3 (KJV) — Commit your works to the Lord.
3. Psalm 37:23 (KJV) — Steps ordered by the Lord.

Chapter 10 — Categories, Timing & Seasons
1. Ecclesiastes 3:1 (KJV) — To everything there is a season.
2. Galatians 6:9 (KJV) — Not fainting in due season.
3. Daniel 2:21 (KJV) — God changes times and seasons.

Chapter 11 — Prophetic Goal Templates
1. Proverbs 24:27 (CJB) — "Put your outdoor work in order…"
2. Deuteronomy 8:18 (KJV) — God gives power to get wealth.
3. Matthew 25:14–30 — Parable of the talents (stewardship).

Chapter 12 — Prayer Points for Divine Direction
1. Psalm 32:8 (KJV) — God instructs and teaches.
2. Philippians 4:6–7 (KJV) — Prayer and peace.
3. James 1:5 (KJV) — Asking God for wisdom.

Chapter 13 — Living in the Overflow
1. John 10:10 (KJV) — Life more abundantly.
2. Psalm 23:5 (KJV) — "My cup runneth over."
3. 3 John 2 (KJV) — Prospering as the soul prospers.

Chapter 14 — Walking in Alignment Daily
1. Psalm 119:105 (KJV) — Word as lamp and light.
2. Micah 6:8 (KJV) — Walking humbly with God.
3. Galatians 5:25 (KJV) — Walking in the Spirit.

Chapter 15 — Rewards of Alignment
1. Hebrews 11:6 (KJV) — God rewards those who diligently seek Him.

2. Isaiah 1:19 (KJV) — The willing and obedient eat the good of the land.
3. Psalm 84:11 (KJV) — No good thing withheld from the upright.

Chapter 16 — Finishing Strong
1. 2 Timothy 4:7 (KJV) — Fighting the good fight; finishing the course.
2. Philippians 1:6 (KJV) — God completes what He begins.
3. Hebrews 12:1–2 (KJV) — Running with patience the race set before us.

Bibliography

The Holy Bible.
King James Version (KJV).
Christian Standard Bible (CSB), where noted.
Complete Jewish Bible (CJB), where noted.

Blue Letter Bible.
Blue Letter Bible Study Resources.
https://www.blueletterbible.org/
Used for Hebrew/Greek word studies, cross-references, and Scripture exploration.

Christian Books & Commentaries Consulted for Concepts and Language (General References):
Henry, Matthew. *Matthew Henry's Commentary on the Whole Bible.* Hendrickson Publishers.
Strong, James. *Strong's Exhaustive Concordance of the Bible.* Abingdon Press.
Vine, W.E. *Vine's Expository Dictionary of Old and New Testament Words.* Thomas Nelson.
Blackaby, Henry & Blackaby, Richard. *Experiencing God: Knowing and Doing the Will of God.* B&H Publishing.
Meyer, Joyce. *The Battlefield of the Mind.* FaithWords.

Goal Setting & Personal Growth (General Inspiration Sources):
Covey, Stephen R. *The 7 Habits of Highly Effective People.* Free Press.

Other Books by the Author

I SHALL TSÂLACH! Prophetic Goal Planner & Journal for Holistic Prosperity
A Spirit-led planner and journal designed to cultivate holistic prosperity across five dimensions: spiritual, financial and economic, mental and emotional, physical, and relational.

I SHALL TSÂLACH! Prophetic Meditation Journal
A devotional journal created to support prophetic meditation, prayer, and Scripture reflection, helping readers record revelation and deepen spiritual clarity.

Daughters of Dominion
A revelatory book awakening women to their God-given dominion, teaching them to pray with authority, walk in purity, and rule from their identity in Christ.

Changing Tides
A timely examination of changes to U.S. immigration laws in 2025, offering insight into shifting policies and their impact on individuals, families, and communities.

Know Your Rights
An educational guide focused on immigration rights and protections, designed to equip readers with practical legal knowledge for navigating the U.S. immigration system with confidence.

About The Author

Loxanne P. Taylor is a prophetic teacher, mentor, and visionary coach passionate about helping believers align their lives with God's purpose. Known for her Spirit-filled yet practical approach to spiritual growth, she equips individuals to hear the voice of God, set Spirit-led goals, and walk in divine order with confidence and clarity.

Her message combines biblical truth with real-world application—bridging revelation and responsibility, faith and focus. Through her teaching, mentoring, and ministry work, Loxanne has guided many to embrace their prophetic identity, discover their God-given assignments, and develop lifestyles of discipline, prayer, and stewardship.

A lifelong student of Scripture and the prophetic, she carries a heart for revival, restoration, and purpose-driven living. Her passion is to see the body of Christ walking in alignment with God and using practical Godly wisdom—believers who not only hear from Heaven but also build what they see.

When she's not teaching or writing, Loxanne enjoys quiet moments in prayer, mentoring emerging leaders, and spending time with family and community. Her life and ministry are dedicated to one mission:

> **To help others see what God is saying and become what He has spoken.**

Call to Action

Your journey does not end with the final page of this book—this is only the beginning. God has awakened something in you, stirred vision within you, and positioned you to walk boldly into the future He designed. Now it's time to take the next step.

If this book has impacted you, challenged you, or brought clarity into your life, I invite you to stay connected. There is so much more that God wants to build, reveal, and activate within you.

Here's how you can continue the journey:

1. Share Your Testimony

Your story matters.
Your breakthrough matters.
Your testimony carries prophetic power.

Send your testimony or praise report of what God has done through prophetic goal setting to:

contact@lptaylorlaw.com

Your testimony strengthens the faith of others and glorifies God.

2. Invite Loxanne to Teach or Speak

Prophetic Goal Setting has transformed individuals, ministries, and even professional environments.
If you'd like to host a workshop, conference session, or Bible study series:

Speaking Requests:
bookings@lptaylorlaw.com

3. Sow Into the Work

If this ministry has blessed you, prayerfully consider partnering or sowing into the work God is doing through Prophetic Goal Setting. Your support helps us equip more people around the world.

Giving Link: $cashlox

4. Keep Building With God

Don't close this book and return to life as usual.
Take what you've learned and put it into action.
Review your vision regularly.
Update your goals.
Pray over your plans.
Stay aligned.
Stay consistent.
Stay surrendered.

**You are not ending a chapter—
you are stepping into a new beginning.**

LOXANNE P. TAYLOR

God has written the vision.
You have made it plain.
Now go and run with it.

Salvation Prayer

God's Word teaches that His promises and spiritual gifts flow from *relationship*, not religion. Every blessing—peace, joy, healing, spiritual discernment, prophetic vision, wisdom, and authority—comes through Jesus Christ.

John 1:12 declares:

"But as many as received Him, to them gave He power to become the sons of God, even to them that believe on His name."

This means that the moment you receive Jesus as your Savior and Lord, you are adopted into God's family. You are no longer a stranger trying to reach Heaven—you become a son or daughter with full access to the Father's love, guidance, and inheritance.

Romans 8:17 says:

"And if children, then heirs; heirs of God, and joint-heirs with Christ."

Everything God gives—spiritual insight, protection, provision, and the ability to hear His voice—is part of your inheritance as His child. But it begins with salvation.

You can't operate fully in the gifts of the Spirit without first receiving the Giver Himself. The "seeing realm," the prophetic, and divine guidance all flow naturally from relationship with Jesus and the indwelling of the Holy Spirit.

Salvation is that doorway. It's the moment you say, *"Lord, I want to belong to You."* Once you enter, everything in the Kingdom begins to unfold.

Salvation Prayer

If you're ready to become a child of God and begin walking in His promises, pray this from your heart:

Heavenly Father,
I come to You today knowing that I need Your grace and forgiveness.
I believe that Jesus Christ is Your Son, that He died on the cross for my sins, and that He rose again on the third day.

Lord Jesus, I confess that I have sinned and fallen short of Your glory.
I ask You to forgive me, cleanse me, and make me new.

Today, I turn away from my old life and I invite You into my heart as my Lord and Savior.
Fill me with Your Holy Spirit.
Teach me to walk in Your truth, to hear Your voice, and to see through the eyes of faith.

Thank You for saving me, for calling me Your child, and for giving me eternal life.
From this day forward, I belong to You.

In Jesus' name, Amen.

If you've prayed that sincerely, according to **Romans 10:9–10**, you are now a child of God:

"If you confess with your mouth the Lord Jesus and believe in your heart that God has raised Him from the dead, you will be saved."

You are forgiven, adopted, and empowered to grow in faith and walk in all that God has prepared for you—including His peace, presence, and prophetic insight.

Final Blessing

May your eyes remain open to see what God is showing.
May your ears remain tuned to hear what Heaven is saying.
May your hands stay diligent to build what God has revealed.
May your heart remain pure, your steps aligned, and your faith unshakable.

You are a visionary.
You are prophetic by design.
You are equipped to set godly goals and live in divine overflow.

Go forward, finish strong, and let your life proclaim:

> **"The vision will surely come to pass."**

Index

Abundance – 95, 111–112
Accountability – 63, 99
Alignment (divine) – 29–35, 71, 103–111
Authority (spiritual) – 44–46, 112
Bible study (prophetic goal setting) – ix, 36
Blueprint (Heaven's) – 22–24, 44
Breakthrough – 52, 95–96
Calling – 7–10, 30–31
Clarity – 1–3, 12–15, 36–38
Consistency – 95–100, 119
Declarations – 44–51
Deliverance – 167–169
Destiny – 14–16, 111
Discipline – 55–60, 95
Discernment – 7–9, 38–40
Execution (of goals) – 55–60, 79–86
Faith – 1–5, 55–58
Foresight (divine) – 14–16
Goals (godly) – 55–95
Habits – 29–33, 95–98
Hearing God – 36–40
Holy Spirit (guidance of) – 36–40, 63–66
Identity (in Christ) – 14–16, 111
Intentionality – 1–5, 55–57
Intercession – 87–94, 152–154
Journaling – 36–38, 127–133
Legacy – 119–122
Meditation (biblical) – 36–38
Obedience – 29–31, 55–58
Overflow – 95–102
Planning (prophetic) – 1–5, 55–86
Prayer points – 87–94

Preparation (for vision) – 29–35
Prophecy – 7–10, 14–16
Prophetic goal setting – ix, 1–5, 55–86
Prosperity (biblical) – 95–102, 111
Purpose – 7–10, 111
Revelation – 7–10, 22–24
Seasons (divine) – 71–75
Stewardship – 29–35, 79–82
Strategy (Spirit-led) – 63–70, 79–82
Testimonies – 52–54
Timing (God's) – 71–75
Vision (God-given) – 1–52
Vision declarations – 44–51
Vision vs. goals – 14–16, 55–57
Vision writing – 22–24, 127
Wisdom – 55–60, 79–82
Writing the vision – 22–24

www.ingramcontent.com/pod-product-compliance
Lightning Source LLC
LaVergne TN
LVHW020928090426
835512LV00020B/3269